Alterworld

By the same author

Alterworld

Sky Poems
The Well Mouth
Alterworld

Philip Salom

PUNCHER & WATTMANN

First published in 2015

Published by Puncher and Wattmann
PO Box 441
Glebe NSW 2037

http://www.puncherandwattmann.com

puncherandwattmann@bigpond.com

National Library of Australia
Cataloguing-in-Publication entry:

Salom, Philip

Alterworld: Sky Poems, The Well Mouth, Alterworld

ISBN   9781922186669

I. Title.

A821.3

Cover design by David Musgrave

Printed by McPherson's Printing Group

This project has been assisted by the Australian Government through the Australia Council, its arts funding and advisory body.

Australian Government

Australia Council
for the Arts

Contents

Sky Poems

Sky Poems

Sky Arrival

Never mind how you got here, or why.
Questions only hurt when the world is apoplectic,
when you struggle a while in doubt. Then die.
You are immortal now. You have everything.
Throw out the world's laws: apples fly upwards
if you say so, twenty angels on acid do a killing,
or make love balanced on a needle. Scientists
discover the fundamental particle, treasurers
balance the absolute budget. But you
are the one, the greatest at everything you do.
Artists work up masterpieces, they are acclaimed
but prefer to make up nasty portraits of their rivals.
Mystics tear aside the veil and look at God, who smiles:
I've been expecting you. Heaven is empty.
And so it goes on. Anything you wish,
possibly more…

Smithy's Dream

This bridge he risks every Friday after the pub.
The hard curve pulls the car out. Something
in the back panics like an animal near the edge.
Tyres set into wild faces by the corrugations,
the body teeters at the apex, this force of G
against his nerves as the sunlight goes up and over.
He sees posts and railing going past like frames of film:
he is the gate moving on the film.

He's never heard of Nietzsche, or the Buddhists,
eternal recurrence, or the headlong return
to the crisis he has once survived. But when
he drives his old Ford onto the bridge
he wants that corner to curve like a black sling
far out and further and faster until the Ford-stone
crashes through the railings
or film flies in a loop away from the projector.
There goes the tool kit skimming past him.
God, what's below? He'll go down into the water
where the lights are always out, where Friday isn't.
Can he pluck the car from after, and place it
before: that side of the bridge before he'd raced it
(and the race an imagery in his blood)?

This one dare he sets himself, the car his will,
and sometimes more than his alone, cornering
without him and succeeding. So
hold it right there. He brings it back.
This time he's modified the rear end (see coloured
roll-bars and new shockies like electric wiring).
And starts again.

Instructions for Living in the Sky

This is the new world: a sphere and its envelope
as blue as you first encountered it: unhatched
from the static of astronauts (so far up, surrounded by darkness)
but held in the metaphors of their white speech.

Blue world. You grip it in your hand,
arm outstretched. It keeps spinning, its oceans
keep their power in strict curvature. But from here
gravity is nothing. It is dream world. There need
be no Newton, no discoveries but your own.

You feel the ancient weight of sun upon your eyelids.
The mountains breathe a mist, the deserts waver
onto their shores. Your sight is swimming
into form, your gaze is daylight.
Peering in you see so much is *green*.
It is the first deception.

You toy with a planet you may have left,
holding it, then, with an exile's hands.
You must create it to enter it again.
Think a box – and there it is:
six-sided, enclosed. It's empty, of course,
unless you fill it: a naked woman,
three constant friends, a set of wings?
You are what you have made of it.

Bodies first: each one transparent as a glass of vodka.
Strip sunsets for the colours, the purples, blood-reds,
the nerving flames. Knead the contours of the organs:
this hand-fruit you hang upon the tree of spine.
Turn it on – disturb the heart, prod the lungs,
transparence runs a torrent of arteries and veins,
red chasing its tail of blue.

They are nothing yet, incredible machines.
They haven't even sex: their see-through organs hang
or rest like held-up water.
                              So now you part that water.
She is startled and re-arranged to feel you enter her.
He stumbles off, runs his hands over his body
suddenly opaque. Their eyes speed up
like an animal's before feeding.

You keep on. Your Dramatis Personae will outdo you
with their dreams and languages. It is only right.
So when you grant them consciousness, when
you fold down into their brains that wild silk
like this blue continual envelope around the world
– pack it carefully, like a parachute.

For you, the same: layers get bundled up,
your concentration's off one moment, your fingers
slip. You do several million in your sleep?
When they need it most, when they jump
(their days will be loaded with tiny practices)
many will discover darkness.

                              So be vigilant,
let mind and finger work together,
remember: the old Zen potter at his wheel
(smooth or rough, a pebble dropped into his mind
is like an asteroid, a thing in space,
the pebble falling).

Protect the beautiful, or admirers who sit in cane chairs
their drinks held perfectly, their accents filled with sunlight,
go suddenly horrendous... kick them down among the cats!
Give people dashings of sex, from crescendos that never stop
to pianissimos. Many will make do with a quaver.
Some take it black without sugar and wearing spurs,
and some by spoonfuls, or like Bach's C Major Fugue
high-heels pressing his hard and single pedal to the floor.

Give them mentations they can do – that are exact
but lesser – they'll call them cities, civilisations.
Sirens that speak in primal languages: the spinal
plunging of air raids, red ambulance fear, fire frisson,
blue police paranoia. In peace, give local signs and signals,
the mathematics of streets.

They'll need unease to counter boredom,
emotions in excess of functions, the voltages,
the AC/DC of attraction and repulsion.
They develop huge obsessions, lock each other up, electrocute
some or all of the body, incarcerate free thinkers
like manic animals they can't quite kill.
It's not the meaning but the voltage that rules.

Release the images that are human art,
the mimicry, the stories they shall know themselves by,
the chance to fix a moment's intensity
like the single needle-point that is addiction, the local Yes
as the concerto falls into place.
Art should strike as lover: rushed, passionate, or
deeply composed – the eye leading back
to that first transparence.

They'll invent theology. They'll invent you.
They will think they have free will, to stand back.
The time will come when they stand back far enough,
arms outstretched – to hold in their hands the small, blue,
relentless planet. Shall you enter it? They'll call you to come.
You'll need all your compassion to refuse.

The Disabled and the Ones in Pain

Have risen from the stubborn world of objects,
their bodies perfect. A sensual weightlessness
operates from the inside out
supporting everything: constricted muscles
the shot-by-shot numbed spines
bodies wracked by spasms
find gentleness, come off the rack.
They live a newer quality, called float,
like the early morning drifts into sex
before you're more than half-awake,
the slow fall of fireworks, near landing
before the next colour-burst. Gravity
was just a state of wakefulness.

The ghost of a missing limb grows back
gleaming, filling out like a trombone.
The blind see their dreams of the world. What *do*
they dream? The shapes of our eyes, or jaws,
eyes feeding along our landscape, curving on
asymetries of people. Some of what they see
will sober them.
A three year-old drifts up from his bed of burns
where adults had to wrestle him, pain the referee.
His infection-saving mask peeled off, his flesh is sane.
But the sky-world cannot explain.

The deaf hear for the first time and some retreat.
Retarded minds begin to spin and breathe,
the veil lifting, the ecstasy, a delirium of thought
as centuries implode on them, though some of this
will keep them serious.
The cancerous purify in moments, tumours
contracting like black stars dragging into them
their crazed and unexpected light. No marks
or signs tell where this anti-life has gone.
No one says it will not visit them again.

Pain-clouds rise above the tortured and the maimed
and all their desperate mantras cure their damage
if not their memory.
Darkness leaves depressives, voices
retract from schizophrenics like broadcasts
swallowed back into the station
to one announcer suave and sane.
But ignorant of much that passes.

So – all wounds gone – new hope waits there
like a brilliant bus, its destination the metropolis.
They rush in, examine each seat one by one,
then settle at the back to watch it filling.
Now they are as perfect as perfect people...
wrenched from their crutches, or their freakdom,
lost from their vengeful or neurotic drives –
what will they make of us who kept them?

Migrants in the Sky

By endless concentration (you feel mad
and look it) it is possible to see their dreams.
Or it strikes by accident, a sudden jolt.
You go like a thief into the darkened house
but cannot lift a single object.
Perhaps you know them, and condescend, being
intellectual, being a sociologist, being well-informed...
They *are* the raw material.
                    The century
falls apart and becomes, absurdly, this locus:
a continental drift in the fractions
dreamt by these survivors, in detail down
to individual streets, intensely-known rooms in houses.
Each dreamer wears a world
like a knock-down film set. Only they will survive it.
Some still wear a World War. Or a Third World,
flame-filled. Or red with sirens ...
Old cities, architecture, laboured stone
a densely shattered music – what is culture but chords
compressed there by the thousand? Let go
now, their universe gapes, and will not
be filled by concrete.
                    Some people
climbed over the gunnels off Vietnam,
and from Islam to the islands, the Indian Ocean.
Coming from the East of broken compasses:
Iraq, Afghanistan, the tears of Sri Lankan jungles,
women, children, men, to live again and none
blow like IEDs in the dust of where they came,
in drowning oceans as they come, in lock-down
when Paradise has been seen for what it is.
Where entire districts crash down, their joints
completely gone.
                    Some simply came.

Remarks about Your Other

Now the woman in red approaches.
Beneath this sky world, she says,
waits another. Everything is absorbed there.
The touch of your hand on another's body
is doubly there – as your touch
and as the pressure on her skin.
Again as the subtle glow and shift
within your brains.
you are being made there.

What you see now, this image of me
is redly there. You looked into the mirror
minutes ago, seeing your gaunt cheek line,
all that, too. The swing of your arm
through air, your speech, the crispness of a grape,
your tasting of her mouth, all the million
nerve-ends of loving have a copy there
in this carillon of the senses,
the scattered traceries of your thought.

Every surface, every object
that receives you draws you down
into your other: the bed, the floor beneath the bed,
the mirror. The utensils you eat with,
the steering wheel, even your desires
weigh exactly down into your other.
Your earth-station, a flattish dish
white with data.
At time you have almost met
this other, a sudden face in crowds
unaccountably shocks you. The instant as your
car turns side-on out of control.
When depression stalks you.

Remember. It is you exactly
but has one difference.
It is laid out in the skin, still as a corpse,
responsive to all you do –

it knows brilliantly as you know in the dull
only one of you can live.
Relentless moments fizzing into the past
annihilate whichever one must live there
perfect and ill.
You must resist it forever.

A Little Bit of Colour

The sky is blue astonishment, a seamless packed blue,
blue hordes arriving billion-fold from all directions
with bursting cases. We're over-run with blue.
Ceramic and china blue, Pollock and that blue about poles.
Blue the flash of fuses, not confused with the oh so
spiritual blue of auras. There is blue-rinse blue,
the sky is an inverted cup (a late addition to china blue)
and the underbelly of Plato's perfect blue.
Erotic films' oh so forbidden blue, the blue of bruises
on a white thigh, speckled bird-egg blue.
Blue floods a peacock's neck, blue finches, blue tits,
blue veins in breasts, and cheeses, blue lips
from the cold, the frightening face of asphyxia blue,
blue after snake-bite, this scary Australian blue.
There is blue blood, heart-pain, left-behind-a-homeland
blues, the Aryan eyes that stared upon the not-so-blue
until the smoke. Balinese silk, batik blue.
The no-home-at-all down and out methylated blue.
There is blue speech from blown gaskets and exhaust pipes
the mechanic's bill blues and then the language.
There is the edge of the cat's milk blue,
the blue rings around the moon, the night sky's
black-blue blue. A baboon's bright buttocks (that's a blue).
Day the diurnal constant in the sky.
And a colour no one is.

Seeing Gallipoli from the Sky

To remember the veterans with my child-illusion:
war had turned their faces white
around the eyes, the skin had gone translucent.
Or consider the days of Anzac in the streets
not only those in suits come back on duty
but the ghosts among their ritual ranks
always in uniform. That or the shock of sepia
of platoons just hours before they left:
that shift across the brain from left to right
from the hemispheres of fact to dream,
like troopships crossed the hemispheres
and left men wondering: was it fact or nightmare?
Without a template of history to hold these images.
They soon got one and nothing could shake it.
Like the enemy it was sudden and total
and like nothing else in the army
it fitted their bodies perfectly.

You see them level and sealed in
or splayed like asteroids
among the dimmed star-shells
or their centres gone like a ring of keys
where they stalled on the slopes and were covered in.
The blown end of a Lee Enfield
makes the weapon seem a crossbow.
There the isolated spine is curved as a bow
the loose ribs are warped arrows
and the earth has kept them close
in its grip and quiver, only sometimes
loosing an arrow in slow and gentle course
out into the daylight.

You begin to mend them. Firstly
you give them back their bodies.
You pick the rosette from a man's chest
pluck each petal of blood and let it drop into obscurity
(there is no copy of it back at home).
His was the famous rush towards the machine-gun pits
but his medals were put too deep, and by the wrong side.
The stem cannot be seen, nor the bullet that gave seed
passing through sternum, heart, lodging in the vertebrae.
And the uprush of bloom into the khaki.

Bruises, those coloured moulds, lessen and are gone.
Ignore the condition of his arteries, whether the joints
gave trouble – they were too young. Your miracles
are for the body and now its dreams,
for these have lapped the gaunt face
like the midnight waves of evacuation.
But there's something arcane about the clay
where fierce Turkish sunlight baked it around his body.
The particles became magnetic, but the magnet's
pulling wrongly: you've stripped his oppressors
from him but he sprawls down facing East:
the light jostling his body, its energetic tearing
calling him to fight – this is where he is intense
this harsher light must be Australia.

He sits up, slowly, exactly as machinery into place,
like a fold-out cardboard shape with savage detail,
the machine-gun straightening up, locking its steel legs.
The sudden racket as shots begin, chronic and nervous…

He will not return as one who went to die well,
coming home like a kind of migrant
strange and unaccustomed, to be made a boy again
– city boy to find his streets
or country boy finding the bright train back
as through the eye of a needle
unthreading his name from the obelisk not yet built.

To grind away Mondays at the office
or the callous-breaking afternoons on land,
dreaming of food through the other war of Depression.
Beside the wireless, monument of the everyday,
strong again, voting conservative
as he mostly would, forgetting violence
until the next war, seeing that one through
or dying again. Or being again returnee to a time
where the world view, his slow meccano
would crumple, seem obsolete.

Three Angles on Absorption

He saw it in the windmill when he went to feed the horses.
She noticed it on walls, and in tutors at universities.
The children heard it in loudspeakers at rock concerts.

One morning it was there, turning but pumping nothing
(the storage tank empty below the outlet). It gave
a familiar muted clank as the pump-rod went up
and over ... the fan spinning like a child-drawn metal sun.
Yet something else turned there, hypnotic spinning.
He was drawn to it, into the blades' inspiratory
whirling. It caught what he couldn't know
of himself. He was wind and this was how
the wind was spied on.

She felt the presence of the walls.
Certainly they absorbed the sound but something else
seemed in wait there, a sensory panel one beat
behind appearances. The tutors were all attention,
one polished and cool behind his glasses, another
too... solicitous even... she felt more than just
examined, it was the silent, insidious absorption.
From her body, the touch of her spine on chairs,
the pressure under her thighs...

They were in the habit, attended often. A rock band
welted in leather: there on stage, black, intense,
their instruments held like flensing knives, slicing open
and taking back. Then beyond those wild guitars
and thrusting black diaphragms, the tower of speakers
just a fronting paradox emitting sound but
gulping more back from the audience
wallowing on the planks like a huge and powerless whale.
Nerves were being snapped on the mixing panel.

No one spoke about it, so separately they suffered it.

Flight: Images from Cartier-Bresson

Every city is a heart pounding and pausing, your city now
or Paris circa '44, Venice, Mexico City, Seville, in Lebanon, Oregon.
But the heart may be more or less disruptive, interfered with
by wars or earthquake, by oppression. By success.
Within all this, is flight.

Paris. The trepan has fallen, the bone is bare:
one absurd wall in a street of rubble, its window
a sightless socket, the same scene either side of it.
Below, three children glide along an edge of pavement,
mid-step, their feet are in the air.
They are smiling. They are at the instant of flight.

Below me the black electric box chatters:
electric cicada of the crosswalk — and the people
wake into movement, feet lifting into space.

Venice. On a rain-flooded sunroof a man who jumped
seems to erupt vertically, the shower of droplets from his shoe
a slipped bracelet that hasn't entered the sheet of water
he is poised above, centimetres, until he lands
where Il Duce is dead, the nation not yet bewildered by elections.

Invisibly, but we know it, in that air,
there's a step everywhere, the same step leads up,
awaits us all, our foot-shock, a flash of white ...
There's a blue opening in the brain — the sky light,
the chute upwards to a place of flight.
Below it we feign to be land livers but for moments
can throw off this delirium of the ground.

Flight is not escapist, or too passionate, not Jonestown
or a riot... Flight is freedom, and yet in service,
it's in zeitgeist and yet a tramp may have it.
Breyten Breytenbach heard it, saw feet lifting with it:
blacks singing the last song of the body before the Afrikaners
hanged them. Its opposite made the young assistants vomit.

Mexico. Prostitutes, eyebrows plucked and pencilled
from nose to temple, arching like wings. One seems
to rise up through her tiny window, out from the two-berth
cubicle with its promises of other flight – men pumping
their wings for these few enamoured seconds.
Nearly closed, her eyes are two pods, her lipstick
perfect, split suggestively on the top lip, her arms
wrapped in to the long dark groove of her cleavage.

Astonished, the Nomad's one passenger:
the plane nearly stalled above the coast the city miniature and white
entering clouds, these rising crucibles
as rain spatters on the perspex. Then all goes gold.
This is flight.

When we're cursed or driven, when anger grabs the spine,
when pain sits in us like a monolith and must be lifted,
when we're blind from depression when the black hour
hits, the final note is written, the gallows beckon,
as the clamps go on the testicles, the blades up women,
flight is pounding like a maddened thing.

Lebanon. Unspeakably, a militia man has it. It is not morality.
As in Gallipoli, in those who played cricket with the bombs
in France, jumping into the open to taunt with opposites.
Both sides have it.

Sometimes it runs amok, or does it satirise?
Leaving a person grounded (but for the eyebrows)
as it makes the table lift a metre high, or
skimming plates around a discontented couple
with that adolescent daughter…
does shifty things in corridors and welcomes the names
of poltergeists. Though they are dead, can't lift anything.

It calls up the hair on the spine or back of the neck,
quite embarrassingly gives fat flight
to that most lively part of adolescent boys.
It's not unknown for breasts to rise. It makes
lovers and ecstatics light on their feet, or backs.

Paris. Old Matisse holds a white pigeon:
the bird has lost it but it rises in his pencil
and in Matisse. It can be transferred. Laughter does that.
If freedom does it, so too the right kind of discipline:
the 80 year old kung fu master runs up walls, slaps the ceiling
three times, then drops lightly as a cat onto the floorboards.

Bruce Lee flying like a rippling hammer, like a flashing simile,
holy men dryly across the river's surface, fakirs with wings,
lamas drifting up mountains, Taoist in full smile across valleys.
Björling and Caruso, who said their voices
flew a foot above them... and in those who listened.

Cartier-Bresson knows how it leaps so much from rubble.
It favours children, lovers and the simple,
all have its brilliant engine.
And in Oregon, railway men trundling an isolated line.
The speed of light setting down those brilliant rails.
You can see from one man's face he is in flight. It wears him
inside out. Flight is images so fast they're stationary
like his velocipede on its spinning wheels.

Paradise

The robed ones: Buddhists, Hindus, Moslems, Jews, those
of Roman, Russian, Greek and Protestant, those suited buckshot
religions of America, abstractionists but not pantheists,
not land-loved totemics — they gather in Paradise.

They pray in corners of this cornerless sky
for the Great Answers, to know the way of crisis:
are they in Paradise, or its Ante-Room, or its Cosmic
Doldrum? Has God hiccupped, choked, stopped breathing?
They vibrate like engines — everyone has the same mantra:

who-are-all-these-others?

They wait. That is, for God, or Gods, or Nirvana.
And their robes are moved by the gods: of wind.
Cloth-deep, holy shapes
                              shifting possibilities of shells.
Their smooth or shaven heads
                              discoloured pearls.
The nuns are wives-of-Gods
                              mothers-of-pearl.

Alms gatherers grope among them, moving slowly
on the wind, annoying all the others with their bowls,
their fossicking-slowed-down of hermit crabs,
claws protruding from their saffron shells.

Where *are* they? Has He or the Buddha-mind
forgotten the street-signs or the entrance-lists?
And the ablutions? This concerns them no less
(heaven must meet World Health Organisation guidelines).
They must squat, their brown mortifications
falling slowly down (at least He has left this gravity)
and disappearing. Until they wonder where it lands…

Archbishops sit in their brocade. The sages
imagine clippers and snip their magnificent beards.
The erudite refuse to speak to the gullible,
and both recoil from the born-again.

On the blue roads leading inwards
are Christians, their foreheads lined with sin,
Hindus calling for servants, fakirs for nails, ascetics
trying impossibly to not be human. Jews, kept down so far
by the great moral weight of being Chosen, have sunk
into depression – some have disappeared downwards
their wails and bitter jokes emerging.

who-are-all-these-others?

Believers sit around, robes billowing with intensities
that are still of the desert. There is no desert here.
But the wind works on them as on tents of the Bedouin.
They squint from the glare of dunes – this flash
of Allah's scimitar, or from focussing down Mahomet's gun.
There are children perfect but for their passions:
folded-up, tied to a pull-through to polish Allah's rifling,
and handed bomb-packs for their lunch in Paradise.
You hear the anguished sounds of martyrdom.

When the Wheel comes, the awesome religious wheel
laid flat and spinning in this spiritual casino:
they must throw one part of their minds on, each chip:
one hope, or fear, or anger, one lust or desire…
and lose them one by one.
                              God is the Anti-Bank
and Anti-Credit. Some, of course, will win,
gaining more than they put on. This is the gamble:
knowing finally their heart's desire.
Here luck is dubious and poverty salvation.

For the first time there is Heavenly Silence.

Speech Making

The room swirls in front of me like wind in a dark forest.
The microphone and stand jut within their chromium forces
as if in traction. This is a sculpture entitled Accident.
I'm dressed in a formal suit. But its perfect fit
doesn't fool me for an instant.

I'm not to speak, yet. There was an introduction
but I missed it, drifting or dreaming.
The man opposite and on my left fidgets in his trousers,
mouths his latest accomplishments, but no one listens.
His face is one of Nolan's miners, in yellow ochre
or is it yellow cake, opening onto macerated teeth.

A woman with massive cleavage has ceased drinking
worried, she mumbles, the police are giving breast tests.
Beside her a woman wears such rocky magnificence on her ears
her lobes are dragged and torn a quarter-inch.

The tables are laden, meals arranged like colours for dissection.
The cutlery begins to shift. I grab for it but it dodges off,
breathes like a set of lungs. A man speaks to me
his lips dropping onto people and place-names
like road signs closing on a major city.

I catch knife and fork and slice down to the bone.
What superb cuisine. This must be dining with the very best.
I would dissect the doubt we live in, flourish great schemes,
but knife and fork make Freudian slips across the plate,
the fish flips away between the breasts of the woman
seated opposite, wriggles there like a schoolboy's joke.

I'm up to speak! Back at the microphone as smokers
release their blue and languorous selves into the air.
Speech sorts out who we are so much better than silence.
So, to begin on what should be the easiest word...

They look at me doubtfully, their faces in three slits
balanced by the nose. Fingers tap along the table edges.
I ... yet before it takes sound, this utterance has shape.
My mouth halts on it like a baby at the nipple,
like a beast above a bone that will be gnawed ...

When the words come they come at last
not like the limbs dragging across that terrible road in dreams,
but like a sprinter's. I stare across
at the clock face, see the dark, unequal thighs
of the old contortionist: Time.
Until the words begin to tire, like particles, their half-life
slips into the listeners' worlds, into each
soft planet nodding there above the plates.

When I leave, someone taps me on the back: 'great speech'
and another 'you rascal, stirred them with that bit about...'
The foyer is cold, the pillars seem out of place
yet as natural as the murmuring crowd. I see the night
outside and down the steps, waiting
like a long soliloquy from a mute.

Epigrams for Performers in the Sky

1
Anything you think of here is real.
Can you think of anything that isn't real?
Can the chess player recognise and call
pieces placed upon the board in chaos?

2
A world lies in place like the lines
of a glib play.
You are amateurs, autists, actors
without any sense of direction.
At times you're like bird-song
without the bird.

3
When any possibility is made real
you sleep beside the slowly ticking clock of freedom.

4
The sky is a computer. You had one text
when you came and used it. Now you have
infinite editing, a virtuoso set of nerves.
Go loose among your incarnations.

5
Here aggressors' victims feel excruciating pain
but don't, in fact, exist.
                    Masochists
grasp every pain but their beaters are ghosts.
Some of you are greedy, real, a bit of both.

6
Beware: I am the huge cloth portrait
billowing from buildings in the public square.
I stare down at you like weather.

Narcissus Considers Himself

It is not enough to live inside my body,
I want leave, to be expatriate, to step
outside its sensual continent.
                            And so I do.
Here is that body, indolent beside a woman.
I ring the changes though: go gold and muscular
as an iron man, or lithe, intense, a sexual Bruce Lee!
I develop fat and am a sumo with round eyes,
or streaked marvellously with green and gold,
my throat pulses, amiable and naked as a frog.
The eiderdown beside us crinkles like spawn.

Nor is it just myself I want to see:
I wind up the two of us, embracing, notice
her breasts loll towards her arms as she lies back
and slowly as a yawn her legs lifting
around my waist...
                        Nor am I without
a sense of fun: my way with mirrors and with
Tiger printed backwards on my buttocks
she can see me romping on the ceiling.
I paint our limbs bright red, so the glass
declares us this vivid two-backed monster
simply one, a spider (she promises to eat me ...).

It isn't merely the body, that like nothing
else in the world is mine (a perfect woman
would give me far more pleasure, perhaps my twin).
It is *seeing*. The fetish of imagery
thrills me, this is the ribald, holy body
where Narcissus lives. Its genitals are eyes,
taking the world in with myself at centre.
It is the double, of viewer and viewed:
lusciously, in an endless silk of seeing.

At times I love the feel of moleskins on my figure
tanned and alone in landscape – the drying outback
drained and ribbed, stretching out before me
like a great wing that has come to rest.

Or I am business-like, a sophisticate, all style –
my body flashes and clicks, draped or geometric.
My hand on a bar-railing stretches no further back
than modern powers, this little history in the millions
just a background for my appearances.

I am a sun lover, my silken g-string just sufficient,
the dark lenses of my glasses the black space
for my gorgeous satellite: she lives utterly
where her reflection curves, given force
by the plunging sling of her bathers.

This body turns, unexpectedly stares
straight at me, I observe what is myself.
The great tanks of my pupils no longer stare
in secret, they dilate until they
merge and gape and I fall through
their terrible waters. I am myself, the bed
surrounds me like an ocean.
The pain is not what I had expected.

Balcony Scene with Variations

She

After two delicious visits by her men, each leaving
smugly on the strength of pheromones, unknowing of the other,
she rests herself back into the long white morning
like a child sick in bed, school day distant
and the fever abating. It is a form of absence
but nothing moves the world too far, nothing is ever lost.
Through the bay window, the blowing curtains, she sees
the balcony constructed of daylight.
                              She is sensual and sated,
the electricity lowered and saved in this long white body
like a toggle-switch, turned off.
                              Until she stands and walks
naked out to where the window throws no shadow,
wearing sunlight more closely than her own skin,
is for those few seconds the cool glissade of atoms
shimmering and intuitive. She is champagne.

He (Il Duce)

His head is a fist, the smaller fingers angled out
to make the taut lips, the chin. Ring-stones
glitter as his eyes. His balcony is a power-rail,
and he is a tyrant.
                  He lowers his stare and inspects
the crowd continually passing. He sustains each of them
their every movement, every slip or tension in their brain.
All day they pass. What has he rescued, saved, or given fever,
that makes them gaunt, exhausted, from praising him?
He twists back to where two pale women wait,
tears their dresses, these frail skins, but fully clothed
his pants just down – like an animal takes them on the floor.
They must stop themselves, to hold his seed as they leave.
His ego won't allow it lost. But already
it is an absence, this cold glissade of sperm.
He stands up, distant as its child.

They

The street is nearly empty. Washing hangs from balconies,
dry as sunlight. An afternoon of shadowed pavements
where life is everywhere, present and distant.
The hours seem turned off.
                                   She flicks a word at him,
he swings up his fist. They glare, darkly,
turn away to lean on the rail. His cigarette shimmers
for a second, then pales. Old now, their gums
uneven, they are slowed down atoms,
the gaunt constructions that were saved.
She finds a curse, but suddenly he seems too frail,
too much a child. Behind him, reflected
in the window, she sees his awkwardly hitched up trousers
and her own skirts, creased as if slept in
during fever. He walks slowly back inside, the day
has made its visit. She sits on, in daylight.

Being There Perhaps, or Not Quite

He's made himself the wall of heaven: salvation's
just the other side of it. But he can't quite picture it.
And so the wall: if you make a wall of heaven
then beyond the wall is it...
                              The argument's exact.
What else is faith? But that's too easy to be that.
He's certain he can hear the saved, mumbling.
And surely he sees across the blue the vapour trail
of Saint Jerome?
                    It seems too quiet. He tramps around
but there's no gate. Halfway over the wall he gets stuck
in cracks he knew he'd wedge his foot in before he saw...
No Saints help him over and God turns his back
as always. Worse, once down, he forgets where he's been.
Remembers for reasons he can't explain – a Friday night,
the mountain air, men in helmets getting him from the car,
then the stipple of bitumen on his back
the pneumatic cutters dazzling as at Damascus.

Beside his wall the trees increase, daylight
shakes down like those ancient spears, the wind
is a green toccata and fugue on Wurlitzer –
(he can hear Bach scream). He has painted the wall
with images of Christ and the Virgin:
they glow in a welter of blues and pinks,
stare down as hugely as Lenin.

His soul enters the bareness of his upper body
his skin as white as milk. And there
all the little pains he's lived through re-visit now
as tiny mutants in his favourite red: bees
visit this skin delicate as blossom, this St Sebastian
– administering their tiny arrows like stigmata.

Oh it hurts, and he fears them as he feared
the daily pains of living (worn now sharp as medals).
These small ones of the holy hive are clearly angels.
He learns the agony of their tiny disciplines
the tiny desolation as they submit to him.
Then resents them: their martyrdom is competition.

But God comes at last to talk to him.
He stands above this body and mind that is distraction,
that has dreamt too much to share its mortification
so is alone in heaven. God speaks the comfortable words.
It's a silly mistake. The martyr wants none of that.
After a stern lecture to the bees, God goes back in.
Heaven is empty again.

Bicentennial – Living Other Lives

At a time when the ruler was troubled by the problems of his subjects, a wise man came to court. He ordered a large bowl filled with water and told the ruler to plunge his head into it. The ruler dreamt of many lives in many places, where justice and riches were plentiful. When he lifted his face from the water, only seconds had elapsed. (*Persian tale*)

1

Which lives shall emerge from the waters? Kelly, the armour
turned back into a ploughshare and all his youth unfallowed,
his gift for language and republic
put down deeply, a furrow across the squatters' country.

Burke and Wills, with their shuffling dreams of continent,
survive and tell, their famous buried food rising in gourmet pods
from the desert, so travellers may keep this side of folly
and know the route of discovery but admit to its transgression.

Aborigines pick out the shot that has sizzled there
like ancestral gravel (a kind they could never guess at).
The boots float back from heads and ribs, bones
find their shape again and the body's country is lived again.

Truganini, King Billy, the taken, reclaim their names, their flesh
from the bare and callous measurers, from the museums'
glass coffins – go back into their place of totem
their white headhunters gone, or utterly uncurious.

A murdered woman (the weighed-down backbone of a nation)
who was left behind the humpy or was it the old white Holden –
minute by minute she counts the bullets in her body
as if they were intimate, then flings them down, having done.

Albert Facey and all his kind, children with their backs
worked bare by opportunists, but now the scars from beatings
gone that were a second language, the universal one.
They its counter-text: rough, naive, unworldly, more profound.

Soldiers return from the mud, the Last Post just missed
as always. These men and women, shock-tourists, loved and drunk,
riotous and a bloody insult to the Empire, thank God.
Awake now to that naive willingness to founder for the British.

And all those young lovers, but mostly fathers and mothers,
who died that invisible death at the wrong end of telegrams
burn now these bitter postcards from another country – the strange
handwriting: 'Wish you were here…' (the picture's blank).

Children rise and breathe again, their skins perfect
and all the sad ways fall from those around them.
The mothers who encircled birth but did not survive it
are themselves born back unto their children.

Women are unraped (the man peeled off like a transfer
or finds every point of contact as he lies over her
burns like a devilish stigmata. She is his electric chair).
She can put the pain aside, the horror finally gone.

2
What will dream of, under the magic waters
where once they were dead and alert, never letting the self die,
or dead in some spiritual sense of justice, this other self
suffering has laid down like the rings of cambium?

There is no new world. They are refugees, heart-people
from the subtle lands of history. They cannot shock-start
in a tea-room, the cup nearly at their lips, or in the Ford, or as
the next brick's laid, at their desk of inventions for watering lawns.

Wipe off the water. The impulse of justice is almost
a new colonisation, the latter century under a pith helmet,
or the great body of a leech that must be turned inside-out
to expel its victims. It is the wish for a whole identity.

All that can be offered is to put them back gently
into death. Where they have felt past rage, indignity,
dishonour. They have gone, as finally as Holt beneath the waves.
A public peace. Only this second death can give it.

The Meeting

They hold their bodies in the strangest ways
Their posture makes them flash like mirrors

I see myself in them leaning forward shocked
I see others caught up or going past oblivious

The answer hits me this implacable face of mine
Is the question of? The world clicks into place

Without a click I move on indelibly within it
Despite the junction of nothingness with my face

It is not the rush of question/answer like a drug
Or two electrode instrument and its narrow pain

But mirrors say nothing is known of such a face
It is the label on this jar of old cigars called self

Can I carry the insight the few hours into daylight?
It bucks inside this question like a poltergeist

Venus — the Lovers

In bed, in front of open hearths — the flames
release this gold and sensual animal —
on beaches, in cars parked under street-lights,
they are naked and making love and shimmering
like satellites.

They topple like a strip show into the audience:
there are bodies everywhere. The air's so charged
it bangs. It's sanguine and split with laughter.
Lovers prowl as smooth as lycra, predators
who hunt into themselves to find a partner,
who make lovers from the memory of faces
the imagery of parts — most gorgeous monsters
(is this what Frankenstein has always been about?).
Or finding another's dream a rough identikit
slip into it, and drift there, being filled.

Taboo is a bumpy road, but here is the frictionless sky.
As for sin — it's an old truck and just won't start.
Earnest ones flatten the battery. Its gloomy fetish.
Yet all their sweaty skin turns something on.
Those who love well, whose lusts are strong and full
and generous, soar up into the sky, or bunt
against the ceilings, their love positions in reverse.

High up their bodies are nearly weightless, they are
Oscar Kokoschka's *Bride of the Wind*. Any positions
are possible, backbones are flexible, organs implausible.
Forget those esoteric pictures in red and green, faces
layered in gold leaf and comic Indian, everyone here
is almost real. Some have used up kohl and Cleopatra
and a man has made up lovers like Byzantine virgins
(but not for long). If the only risk is altitude, the orgasm
short of oxygen is meant to thrill, or keeping on and on
they might explode...

But cruel lovers, insincere lovers, lovers who fear sex,
grow heavy, their doubtful acts accumulate like bodies.
Their genitals are like return keys, each touch on them
calls the sum of heaviness and they plummet:
too heavy for the sky. Their bodies press behind them
like Duchamp's nude descending the staircase.

No little death for them,
their little death is *not* to come:
thudding into sides of buildings, splaying in trees
or trellises, earthing out in a sharp blue flash.
The earth absorbs their orgasm. They don't deserve it.

Some lovers seek the perfect partner, loving as equilibrium,
find steep peaks and tipping back of one-handed love,
and drift off, disappearing into their Cheshire grins.
Greedy ménage à trois skate sideways, skittish
and inclined to roar.

Here the jealous
lack imagination, who normally have too much:
see every burning love-mark, hear every lick and whisper
(resentful imagery weighs them down).

Some want to love but wear the act
too poorly, clinging where lust is a kind of vertigo
and orgasm is a quiet and only sometime friend.
They keep to old routines, the clumsy game of skins
they will stay wrapped in, murmuring and thin
as the wind loves them, blows them end over end.

Oh lovers… Sunrise plays its down upon your bodies.
You are naked or the clouds are sudden lingerie upon you.
The sky is a long blue tongue that trails along your thighs
until you skim, gleaming, phosphorescent, into darkness.

He Sees She Sees

He is five foot two, and as thin as a paper clip.
He tries out several great shoulders in a white suit,
he is brown and muscular as a horse.
She is tallish, stooped, she has a horsey nose.
She straightens up, increases in voluptuousness,
strides like a model, her face immaculate and poised.
He notices her admiration, well, what woman could resist him.
In fact she is trying different heads on all his shoulders.
She sees his stunned look, hears the catch in his voice.
He is worried she is flat-chested, her lips are porcelain.
A gentleman, he opens the door, his Porsche's black enamel.
She spurs up the horses in her Lamborghini Murciélago.
They drive like racers, absorbing lust from their passengers.
He goes to his place, she goes to hers.
She's fed up with subterfuge, tears off her clothes in the bed.
He professes knowledge of all kinds, strokes her like a cat.
She is dressed again, in silk, prising confessions out of him.
He makes love to her as no woman has seen.
She makes a scene and thinks it is love.
They have oral sex because she loves that special feeling.
They have oral sex because he loves to see it happening.
She's still going, still coming, still changing.
He's stopped, shocked, changes back to himself in confusion.
She screams, seeing him thin, along that awful nose.
Such is her shame, she could almost break him.
He chokes, seeing the horse he's been riding, struggles
into a tacky jacket. She scoops into an ancient petticoat.
He roars off in his Holden, she rattles in her Datsun.
Both bend over the wheel, scowling.

Through the Open Sky Window

This is the sky room. There are my two windows:
one is open and a tapping comes from the other so I open it,

fall back just in time (there's a chair exactly convenient)
as the rush begins – plates, handlebars, a pair of socks,

landscape paintings, biros, jackhammers, radios – one of each
but drained of colour, all of them a ghostly white –

two hitchhikers, desks, elephants and Indian rider, trees
that really tax the window to its limits. A pale tractor…

This random debris from the world of accident flows
in one window and out of the other, perfectly ordinary

it seems, this room a T-bar to the endless Milky Way.
But what to make of it? Familiar and yet desolate, no use crying

over spilt debris, tins of ham, two lovers locked in orbit, gleaming
and phosphorescent (hardly NASA or the Cape, they are chased

by those desperate objects from sex shops). A chair with three legs
falls and stands like a war veteran, and having said that, here

is a war veteran, his face no longer creased or anguished.
A Mercedes tight as a skull, man crouched in it like a hermit crab.

Square-shouldered suits, a woman in scraps of Pierre Cardin
(they cover her navel and cling to her right hip, her left breast,

otherwise she's naked but she cat-walks and she's grand).
Some bony hipsters tumble in, young and over-excited

their shirts and pants a tight new fashion, and slipped on
to go out forever. A stream of books, some burning,

blazes past, one or two falling: a manual slowly fans open
but out of date, it's worthless. A woman, proud and alone,

and one of them done in by Edgar Cooke – she's been travelling
these slow decades in search of resolution. And for him.

Accident had her shot, like slippery roads or cancer, his mad eyes
looking for a late light to shoot at. If it's not their dream I see

it's someone else's, they'll wake from it into another world.
But which? Or what? Here comes crushed furniture, a sleepy cat.

A poet drifts through, perhaps he dreams me dreaming him
but he's knocked flat by a gang of kids and a man staggering

in T-shirt only, drunkenly searching for a flowerbed
to piss on. China ducks, loose at last fly from their wall.

What is randomness? Are these messages of a grand design?
A suitcase filled with postcards of some great event?

A terrorist leaps in, both fists blazing, some Persian roses,
a child with cancer. This song of Mahler by Janet Baker,

just for me Jussi Björling and Thelonious Monk,
a high-pitched Chinese cook floating among his satellites:

cleaver and chopping board, spices and wok, and a million
juggled dishes, then a single clerk grumbling with his pages.

Can I step to one side and disappear? A man drifts through
pointing to a higher room, the view better, the windows bigger.

But who affords a penthouse? And why is the lift so often locked?
Daily it goes on – one of everything, between my sill and transom.

My half-Ark that never fills. And the more I try to wake from it,
to feel the sun on my face, the more I sense the water flooding.

Sky Creatures

The Hermit Crab

Despite the ocean going bankrupt
its business — is business:
this creature moves all day in the shell
of a glittering Mercedes.
                    It eats new schemes
from phone and blue-tooth, navigates
millions that fall into its lap like larvae.
It smokes cigars as thick as CEO bonuses.
The world would cease without it.
Who else has underwritten the world?
Or weighed so exactly each transaction of daylight?

The Slandermander

Is amphibious, lives in a watery truth.
Speaks up from the murk it finds
in the kicked-up waters turning black
of grease-banked Australian rivers.

On the rocks it is mud-skinned
reptilian, gladly cold of blood. Strangely
its underbelly is the colour of skim milk.
Often it changes colours: keeping in
with its company. It may seem
solid as furniture, but its upholstery
leaves a stain.
                    In fact
it's all that's left of a cousin's line:
Tyrannosaurus. Too small for fronts
instead it gnaws at backs.
Sometimes it prefers the dead.

The Trumpeter

This isn't lost, but loses itself on purpose.
It is roundish and smooth, eyes shut.
Alone it is useless. Air passes into it
then out through the instrument and across to us,
air swirling in, pushing hard inside the body
as together they push against the trumpet
and the music. We're left with the sound
of air being bent out from the bellows
like red-hot metal by a black-smith.
It blows until its skin is hot and humid.
It blows until its face is a red birth.
It blinks open to a swaddling of applause.
The brass licks its gleam around the bell
back into itself. The trumpeter goes all soft.

The Writer's Table

For days on end the tyrant
bends the table down with his elbows.
Its lungs are under pressure:
breathing is so difficult
it has never taken up a sport,
it never leaves the room for a walk.
It stares into the mirror
seeing a reflected world there.
It presumes this is reality
but then unaccountably
it suffers estrangement
like an invalid or convalescent.
There are things to say. It would speak
only it is inhibited.
Its words appear on the page.

Portrait on the Fourth Wall

I catch myself again – prodding the air between us
like a punchy politician
keeping the argument one way.
Our subject is each other, as long as words will grip.
It's a rough art – arguing
that arguing's essential, authentic,
but watch it topple to a last ditch anarchy
like knocking down a losing game of chess.

We're still at it as sunlight
blazes in the missing wall.
She's in profile, gold and tense,
charged as synapse.
She's a Bob Fosse mannerism
(if we were simply lovers
you'd see the back-lit thread
of saliva between our lips).

Something sinuous and lithe
twists through us, a long tendentious logic,
the muscle of certain words.
It's the other side of domination, but
far more intimate. Our daemon epiphanies:
so I'm the bastard she's usually avoided…
she's the bitch they said she was…

We're disgruntled lovers, drinking our blood clarets.
I'm training up another lust, anger
coming from the greater circuit
where voltage is a karmic gravity
pulling her down. She knows that I'm
that prickly Ancient, I wear her,
gold albatross around my neck
and fix her with my glittering lies.
She is both my curse and my multitude.
We know this navigation far too well.
Oh the painted ship, its
circum-marination of the brain!

The wall? I knocked it down,
let in all the wandering races. I want them all.
They come with food and clothing
with whisky stills, with chatter, with camels
and prayer-mates, with wild music,
with plans for irrigation.
We contain this multitude like a crowd
electric on a hot night.
There, I say to them, there she is,
do you know what I must do?

By nightfall it's the same.
She smokes furiously, I drink.
The ceiling's wild with smoky hieroglyphs
her wit is hardened to tungsten
her beauty is a rage inside my body.
But the argument stops. For seconds her face
pitches on regardless, a lip writhes...

Only now I see the operator
behind her with the grips and levers
cranked over so her arm goes up...
I'd thought it was tiredness, a shadow... No,
her face splits awkwardly in the mouth,
the straw-like handful of hair seems obvious.
No. No. She wrinkles and folds
across a line where her breasts begin.
She is packed up, put away. No!

All night I have argued with a *puppet.*
Plastic, padded out, three-quarter size
(I'd thought she was *petite*).
The operator smokes a cigarette – I'd seen it before,
intensely scarlet, thought it was a planet
back in the darkness where the wall isn't.
She stares at me for just a second, then leaves.
My arms are waving hopelessly.

Contraries in a Modern World

Culture is like a spectrum, built within the range we see.
Dreams, you say, are imagery of a higher kind. Perhaps.

I drive to a new place, the buildings condition me like music.
An acquaintance I suddenly recognise years before I could have
shows instalments of my life, says with exercise I can improve it.

And does the brilliant figure and cool wit of the girl behind the bar
equal knowledge of higher faculties, applied like her purple lipstick?
She looks at me like that, yes, that. I feel I've been screwed.

I shift back to what is past. My memory – ah – the oldest friend
fits me like a deep coat. Yet pockets gape where before they just
weren't... Hands thrust in them I feel for once dressed perfectly.

But I feel not unlike Rip Van Winkle wandering changed streets.
Everyone tells me I'm as old and dreamy as a derelict building.

When, finally, I catch sight of myself in a darkened window –
I see an once grand house, but its tiles are broken and slipshod.

Wandering the Sky

Astonished I see what some will not let go.
A quiet couple standing, a 'ginger' purring on her shoulder,
washing flapping on the line, the world empty behind it.
There is a secret room, dark and esoteric
where the one machine spins on under labour.

A woman has brought her boorish husband,
preferring this than face the yawning white front door
and the sky behind it that is her freedom.
She winds him up like an old gramophone,
the chromium arm coming over, shrieking.

Here the sky is stuck at 9.15, desks and screens
stretch into the distance like grave-heads at the Somme,
the dream is uniform and dazzling white
bent over them. Latecomers are scolded like children,
begin emails like the protocols for sending emails
and get no further. The first job shudders into them
like the first strong drink.

There are artists who throw their stuff like mud:
blobs of colour burn like meteors towards the planet's
white and whirling canvas, certain of a masterpiece
if any of it lands. At last, so fiddled with, they hate it.
Writers three parts way through lines (and whisky)
turn sour-eyed, paralysed by revisions.

Suiciders measure out the pills of transformation
or find the weapon's unequivocal edge.
Some deaths remain as was intended, the gaping
apparel of revenge. Others find it measured
exactly to their guilt, wear it close upon them.

I wander the sky, confused... But
when I ask them what they want they say
'We want our freedom.'
Shaken, I turn away.

Epigrams Again

1

The world performs to us and we to it,
from lyrical to savage give and take.
Any point is indeterminate.
For everything we give, its thought
comes first, like a white curtain
blowing bell-like into the bedroom.

But who or what is the wind?

2

There is a woman with a gun, she has written poems
but now she shoots down rows of men.
They knock down like tin ducks at the shooting gallery
then flip up again at the other end.

3

Don't think there is no drama
between the acts you dream
and the dulled-out concept
of yourself. All is erotic:
you want to live your life
and be voyeur of it.

Three Dreams of Destruction

1
Some cell in him begins to dream:
that demented one standing on a bridge
searching the darkened city for a stranger's light still on.
Delivering his late mail, straight, hot from the barrel
when the door opens.
                        He makes people
in adjoining cells – this is the old brain's factory –
the doors still open between two hells.
Which will be aggressor, which be victim?
His mind dances – Shiva-like – huge erotic tensions
bristle his hair on the nape of destruction.
He shakes like an electrocuted man.

One by one, he places them in the street.
Their cheeks bloom with smoke, oxygen's blue thread
winding through them. He has made every kind,
the fat the thin the muscular, the arrogant
and all filled with ruin.
                        But when it comes to action…
This one has a mole beneath her nose, this man
stands there painfully, favouring his left leg,
another man has three-days' growth, and smiles,
two children pull faces behind their parents' legs,
this woman's lips are surprisingly full,
this man's arms and legs are natural assets.
Even this man's ugliness is a thing in itself.

He tells them why they're here. But he's given them
personal histories, couldn't bear their animal blankness
and their bellowing yells. He has made them too well.
They turn on him *their* bitter gaze.
Their faces abrupt machines, they are almost silver.
They want revenge – it is the other side of justice,
concept pure as the blood shifting in their veins
after the oxygen has bubbled off.

He sees them
black silhouettes in rows like
black targets at a shooting range. But still he cannot
turn on them the sudden rifle at his cheek. The light
shines aridly behind them, their features gone
into compelling profile, black against the agony white
of the street. Then silver again.
                    They move towards him.
It is the made thing not the maker that inherits.

2
But somewhere it happens:
strangers dragged onto the street, or from upper storeys
the hands that pushed, stay fleetingly, then like a sneer
draw back into the darkness, exactly balancing
the street-ending screams of the fallen.
A child is torn until it sags, emptied of its lively steam.
A woman is grabbed, the violent worry of her clothes
until she is wrenched apart like a fresh loaf
and men fall on her. The victim is sometimes known.

This hatred is not personal – that is more intense
and more forgiving. Perhaps. This is blunt, mental,
like bees dreaming of hexagons, all shape
but no perspective, until joined up in a mob.

Bullets splash onto a group of people, Hollywood style:
a white shirt erupts in a row of red blossoms.
You see, slowly, bombs exploding in a yellow blast-line
but must imagine what is happening below them,
Allah's children back-packed to explode in crowds
and buildings. School books carry their heart-flowers
from the traumatised stem.

The wrong mythology is always at hand. Civilisation
waits there, off the streets. All the dead, perhaps,
are re-made there. Naked, their nudity immaculate
and as sudden as tiny frogs after rain.

3

Some men love their archetypes,
the sword fight (for those with a razoring or stabbing fetish)

or machine-gunning (the blast and recoil, fast co-ordinated fucking)
or the brawl (Bruce Lee phallic thunder of feet and fists)

you're pushed as far as you can go – the mob's
got your sister or your girl and you've been slashed.

You must disorder yourself. Find the noble switch
that makes you killer. Somehow it makes you glow.

You win though (of course), body taking its superficial wounds:
they fall back from you and down like a chequered flag.

You are the hero, you feel the crowd within your body,
first the blood-shaking power, then its wild adulation.

Women swoon for you. You're weary, silly as a drunk.
Like Picasso's brush, inspiration goes no further up

than the genius of wrist. Your weapon has done for you.
Tame, you turn like a bird, preen a troublesome feather.

You stay with the bodies. They lie there, inert, unscathed.
Amazed you see they are your neighbours, parents.

Or lovers, friends, acquaintances … dressed in the everyday
casual, nothing fancy. Ah, you're just a simple lad at heart.

Night Under the Sky, a Repetition

S overcomes the habit of going inside. This compulsion
under starlight takes over from the yellow window comfort,

the warm undertow of house. It waits there like a loyal dog.
He thinks the night has knowledge, intuitions that

infect him as naturally as a virus. The sky is a rash of stars
and he is its skin. It works in him like anti-body

against that which drags at him, to succumb, to enter
the house again. He knows what's there: true skin

and the rash of surfaces, the rash of common things.
Where life is specific if not exact. Prosaic as a plate.

That is enough to stay outside, to endure the cold of night,
the cold precision of stars. Ancient, intermittent, it

almost speaks, without delirium or heat, it enters like a needle
of consciousness, a fire within the old crate of his nerves.

The Mysterious Song of the Telescopes

Night breathes like a black saxophone
and night-birds cry out naked as trumpets.
But from light or the dying of light
comes a longer vibration. Stellar notes
riffle our intellectual senses; here is cool
star-jazz – the hiss of the brush on cymbals,
planets crooning *I am Venus I am Mars*.

Some are no more than brilliant metronomes,
classicism from brassy suns. Some have drunk so much
their livers have swollen, then fallen in.
It's the spaced-out lifestyle, the electric road.
Yet it was current before the earth was
and will outlive us. It's esoteric and intense
(before we made the words) a shimmering sense.

Tiny upturned sensors in our minds
know it each long night: facing up at skies
filled with glinting instruments. Below, it's closer –
glossy in a loved-one's hair, or travelling the years
as silver streaks appearing in the blackness.
This is where the light goes…

Poets are obsessed with it, astronomers
who make a cult of light, and no less its rhythms.
Wondering where it goes when it leaves the body
completely, make titled instances written down,
impelled towards the source exactly as they left it.
The sky just lets it happen.

Everyone dreams of it in metaphors:
the latest model gleams of it in baked enamel,
fame, fortune, our name in lights, and on the tongue.
Thinking we've got it, whatever it is, when we
haven't, imagining, most desperately of all, after
suffering there must be light for our flawed selves
picked up by some telescope…

Perhaps we stare too closely, we can't resist,
hearing the sound of quarking,
seeing like Paul Klee graphology
straight-and-curved-line ghost prints
of bubbles in cloud chambers
(duck-diving at speeds of light). Angels
bring the host of thin neutrinos — as if there
was God's laughter down small.

Walking at Night

We roam the streets at night, lovers
heady with perfumes: here are the lushest gardens
where nothing rots or grows still.
We've made each street again and again: precise
as childhood. Streetlights glow overhead
like the teeth of a huge zipper; the universe
steals in when the zipper's open. At the end
is the brilliant villa upon the hill,
where the world ends. I do not know what it is.

After days of love, argument has wrenched the house,
brawling makes the air spark and the bloodstream
seek its questing. We draw back from the hill.
I walk to the house of my mistress where we pool
attention on our bodies, stick pins in our marital secrets
then wander naked in her desert, looking for answers.
Returning, I feel unspent euphoria. Its place
is the brilliant villa upon the hill
where the world ends. I do not know what it is.

The pleasure of returning is to rebuild.
The same materials never lie in the same way twice.
We are a family sifted by days. Nothing is still.
We cleave together like tender and crazy tapestry
sewing images with deft or indifferent movements
then reaching back, repeating what doesn't suit us
until we get it right. I include my fear, it
is the brilliant villa upon the hill
where the world ends. I do not know what it is.

We are sped against our friends, decide to win.
Make another country and return. She runs off to kill
a weakness, but finds her own and stays until the sun
fades upon her thighs. I get drunk with friends, shout
up revolt in a room filled with publicists. By morning
both of us are famous. By midday our children are grown,
by evening someone had died. My answer
is the brilliant villa upon the hill
where the world ends. I do not know what it is.

River River

1

See the water. Dragonflies speeding and breaking back
to hover-still... What power rests there, behind

those compound eyes. The river blinds me to the lower level
glare that covers darkness. But above all this I see

the blousey ripples made by the wind, the twigs
jettisoned from trees. Rising above the banks

rows of white houses, their long private jetties
gleaming with launches. Here are the driven piles

of money, domination's vain root in the river.
This is the unconscious: boats knocking against piles.

Or pleasuring to spin and scream upon another river,
to charge upon its ruins, revving up, and back

to gash the upturned face, to lacerate the chest,
the glittering limbs. Passivity is all the rage, forever.

I see Phlebas, the Phoenician, a fortnight in the wake.
This is the new world on the make. We have no history.

The boatman is not on call. He shipped his oars
long ago, for props and jets. Their cavitation won't stop.

Two women drape drowsily on the launch's bow
beside the chrome eye-blindness of the rails.

Men stand behind dark glasses on the bridge.
They swap and boast, only their fortunes to worry of.

2

Moonlight intensifies the sound and sight:
birds and insect improvise
above the gentle keyboard of the river.
There are lamps and murmurs
of people, hidden like viewers in the cinema.
Moonlight intensifies the sound and sight:
the river passing stark and sensuous as film.
There are those who fish, wanting this night
the line at least under tension.
Or playing simply for the sound, of the reel
like a cicada, winding in.
Moonlight intensifies the sound and sight:
but some are here to worship,
make no mistake about that, though how,
or whether they even know it —
unlike Siddhartha who lived expressly by the river
just to find it — is irrelevant.
Why should the intuitions of the night
keep alive the day tomorrow and its night?
Moonlight intensifies the sound and sight.

Fifty Storeys up into the Sky

This must be a hotel room, he is surrounded
by the traveller's continuum: a bed, lounge, kitchen.
But he sees only kitsch: the light fittings a bouquet

and a gush of glass. The un-matched chairs hunker
like animals abandoned at the food stall.
They stare up, emptily, at him.

He turns the TV on. Its images collide in showers
bearing down an alien sense of where the screen
is a flickering wound, a slick hallucination.

It's cold and hard as a lunatic, and just as draining.
In the bathroom, porcelain white or steely gleaming
basins and shower: two eyes of blue and red,

a mouth that strains to speaks but only murmurs.
His fluorescent face in the mirror is robbed and wan
as a pallid oil portrait. The lines, worse, not his own

on this spare body – suddenly he has woken up
as Sam Beckett! Hair on end, face all cracked and open
but not a play in sight. The self has left his body

by the balcony: so staring down he falls momentarily
but feels the upward lift into himself again. Again.
Later, in bed, he listens to the notes, atonal music:

the radio above the relentless bass continuo of city.
Miniscule waves move in his whisky bottle. Here the city
and planet reinforce, or cancel. Which, he cannot tell.

Like old mad Newton, adrift among minutiae, in his room
fifty storeys into the sky. Light travels through the curtains
late and low into an empty glass, ending outside spectrum.

Sky Travelling with a Sunroof

The highway is endless. The trees rear like gelled hair
from the razed edge of a New Wave hairdo.
You are the rich one driving without effort.
You rest among the dials and gauges
and the dashboard of your white Mercedes
gives back its pure order, its metaphors
of profound machinery.

Each gap between the trees is the sunlight's
staccato drumbeat. The sticks
are long and gold and motionless:
you are the skin, moving and hit repeatedly.
Perhaps it's this insistent jazz – something
at the driver's side, the right of the brain:

you see thumbing beside the road – and stop
to let in smoothly upon the lamb-skin – a woman.
You ignore her sweat, the long slinking smell of her
her long day of hiking, or maybe making love,
for she is naked upon the covers and the seat belt
parts her like a long deliberate tongue.
You are beside yourself with attraction (keep driving)
the sun still beating at your temples.

From her shoulders now, rush instantly, complete,
two stunning wings, more brilliant and more
sensual even than her silken perfect body.
Only now does your endless spin and circle, your
driver-love of the wheel, falter and swerve.
You fill up with nostalgia. It's all you can do
to keep the car clumsily onwards
while the old world hurts you and beats there
bewildering and extraordinary, in her wings.

You turn to where sunlight on her coppery skin
flares and flames into a man who locks her
in a naked love-knot. Her feet rise on the sun-rim
of your dashboard, ten-toed and primal

among the sober dials. Even your instruments
begin to waver! Your speed is less and slowing.
They indicate your life in stages showing
certain losses, going red then slowly dim — you ache
to fill the absence, to begin your life again.
But this is lust you travel, and you are chaste.

He offers her, and her smile, to you but you're in shock.
She glows as she envelops him, so bright you look away.
When you turn back they are women, naked, veined
in the heat, caressing each other like Escher's hands
each tracing out the other's shape.

The road is darkening. The car is empty except for you.
A hiker looms ahead — the face vaguely unfamiliar —
it is yourself. Except you leave
her there, startled, drive desperately on.

Detached and in the Manner of a Veterinarian

Down, as if the sun weighing upon her back
collapsed the angles: a cow's geometry
of spine and pelvis and tail bones
like a flooded yacht, the mast flattened from bow to stern
and the sails stretched taut across the deck.
She labours and wallows but the storm is within,
and is womb-gripe, and the sun is within
that will not sit right, will not accept
what shunts a calf out into daylight.

It couldn't be that nothing was being born,
that if I reached in to put it right I would
drag out what isn't there or is before its time.
Somewhere in this act, the thing is being born.
I reach around and find the first parts
which must be legs, followed by the bulbous head –
but there's something strange about the form.
And after the rope and my rhythmic pulling
there slops out the completely startled shape:
like a calf in its glistening bag
falls the whole, wrapped continent.
I leave it on the ground, with its fabulous lines,
its hybrid colours, its seven unequal brains.

When I return days later, the thing has found
a kind of motion, rushes everywhere on the mania of legs.
I see the cow has two tails, the long afterbirth
she won't let go. When she's in the shed
I reach into the ferment, along the twisted sluice-rope,
find those ardent fingers in the womb's placenta.
I hear voices and demonstrations, the cow
is hot as argument yet blank in her face. This end of her
is not her, but I feel the cotyledons grip like vices
and the talk is all the time condescending and disagreeable.
I reach deeper, I peel and release.
It feels like a flag, but spilling out are hands, loose
and everywhere, hands. They flicker on her hide

like flames. She lumbers off. The calf is twice as big.
I look down at my own hands —
they're smudged with the flame.

In no time the beast has grown huge and flat,
covers the entire continent. The coastline fits
like a glove. This is what it will inherit,
as the land becomes this now, its age
covered over in the flame of hands.
I hear life bellowing in it. I hear death.
I can't decide what my place is here
except to speak of this. The beast remains
sensitive to the powers of speech.

The Locust Journalists

These are bulbous bodies with time in their arteries.
Each mind is a slowly opening concertina.

Hear the facts gasp in through rows of tiny holes.
This is the great brain breathing.

They are insects of vantage-point: not flight but swarm.
The best are analytic. The worst make do with nerve.

They drift above the long hallucination of the world.
Like poetry their forms are compressed, selective.

A poem can get it right by being wrong.
They can get it wrong by being right.

A Cosmetic Surgeon and His Closest Creation

She doesn't even smile
as he enters her. Her lover now is anaesthetic
and *he* is power: all his speeches are
... of beauty. But his scrutiny, astringent.
This is her fourth time under.

She sleeps. The knife worries her
not at all and never does she feel
its hunger – this clean-toothed parasite –
make her less. She is the inner block
becoming: Michelangelo's emerging figure.
The modern version, advertisers' dream,
the lone body in the voyeur's
gauntly fingered corner.

He is Eguchi in Yasunari Kawabata's
House of Sleeping Beauties and she is the girl
drugged for his evening's pleasure. And she
dreams of it, foolishly, under his sun.
It is hot from concentration, the heat laid
like a Mayan wall, and so too her beauty,
shaped, invisible blocks seamless when
finished, when he lays the scalpel down.

They wait, as always, for the healing.
When she poses, she is asana and after-point
of his Yoga. But her breast is too low on the right,
the nipple slightly squinted (unlike eyes of portraits
that follow you around, hers almost wink).
He stares at her, strangely, when they make love
or leans across the breakfast to touch her mouth.

Just when he gets her right he'll notice
scars (she showed the cameraman, beside the pool)
silver gleams beneath each breast, upon her legs,
here and here, where his restless eyes
(like fish hooks) grazed. Tinier than
stretch marks but crossing her body; their
pattern, like the under-surface of a swimming pool,
wraps her in its silver nets.

(Imagine your face before you were born, he says.
Remembering some koan from the Buddhists.

She says I'll remember you the next time round.
The chopping board questions the cleaver?)

Bar Sonnets

1

The spirits stand like midgets, each squat chrome bladder
in place, each tiny prick, the slab-backed men all facing in.

Here is the dark-room, windows opaque, lights snapped on
at opening as the world retreats and the trays swim...

Certain words are regular, touch points, voices going smooth
as leather at each trouser loop. It's home and country wisdom

by these ironists of the public bar: having no use for time
they're stuck with plenty of it. But the talk is tightly buckled,

it holds up, holds in, though heresies have a place in it.
Any speculation, except if it's too clever. They talk of skill

and the lucky bastard with it, like something big behind the zip
but its kept pretty level and sounds like somebody else.

It's a language not of heroes, but about them. In silent moments
their eyes move on the barmaid with a kind of pain.

2

Swaps the bum and stool years facing the bar
for a three-sided frame to stagger with —
stroke, incapacity, sobriety, his alloy partners.
Worse than careers that have petered out
pub-life wasn't planned for highs and had them
best by accident. It was enough to be constant.
Posters against the wall: race winners since '48, league
premiers since '60, footballers whose massive arms
are roped across a past that is no less than present.
Dying was talked of lots, but illness was the fear.
God, he says, liver like a football, brain like a boiled testicle,
just when the see-throughs came, breasts as gold as beer
I felt like a stallion on the fourth card but nothing moved in the stalls.
My body's no good where I'm going. My mind was no use here.

3

He can't decide which is best: splitting the pack to win
like a bloody hero, as a god in this godless world —
or talking about it later. He keeps his age, but he plays
young and brilliant, his talk is middle-aged, but full of power.
Each word is muscle, every conquest shines with sweat.
He'd had a flash of winners, the notes flash like a manuscript:
biographies of Aussie heroes. Again, and again? His face
lets it slip. And the audience knows it.
                                        He feels power
where they pull him now, wanting his balls for themselves.
Feels it going. Like Christ, he says: don't touch my clothes.
Though he takes them off for screwing women, he is shrunk
being naked, even if his prick's bigger than a bat handle and
she's onto it for a century. Can't dream anything more sensitive.
His dreams ride shotgun, brash but scared, guarding him.

The New Fatigue

Heroes stare into space, pick their teeth.
Heroines file their nails to the slow.
Tightrope walkers refuse the next success.

Their feet have moved so full of instinct
naked on the wire like snouts. Depressed
by this long sky sagging between posts.

Torturers relax, bored by throats, genitals,
skulls tilting about their feet, their captives
slumping nude and mute as mushrooms.

You see them struggling, but something awry,
players who have found their perfect author
but have forgotten how to act.

Knowing their heart's desire delivered
so bluntly, on and on, and ... Ah, sets
of brilliant clothes dreamt every night.

In the morning drawn on, the trousers
too revealing in the crutch? The shirt
a parody of chesty Charlton Heston's.

So retro, after all: fantasy's nostalgia.
You consider dying in the first scene.
Drinking a goblet of bloody ennui.

Surging through its orgasm or torture:
leaves you sated. By heavens and hells
of the blood. Dante played by de Sade.

Trumpeters play short of final notes, hang
off harmonics and won't resolve, fearing
extinction. Older lovers refuse to come.

How utterly sick of everything
everything is.
            Tired even of seduction,
the seducer.

What Is Made?

The old Zen monk
rakes the sand garden
surrounding the rocks
the sand is the pattern
the pattern is the sand
this one man being so
meticulous in this one
man meticulous about
being

With no sand garden
the old Zen monk
(are they always old?)
misses its rough edge
daily he pushed from
out into nothingness
his mind the old rake
his breath on leaving
like a row of pebbles
he is pushed from

With nothing outside
everything within
making a new world
to empty the old one
all similes locked up
now let out again
this first intelligence
of poetry stroking
all the right places
emptied even Buddha
as usual to kill him
again the rough world
to push away from

The World of Dreams

The world of dreams
is no salvation
no one lives in it
except the mad
who are sane there.
It is our half-life
by which we balance
and is replaced
by art and memory
against all better judgement.

It is wiser than us
but has no manners
it's as modern
as modern poetry
and always has been
it's as ancient
as cave paintings
and always will be.
You can fly in dreams
enter minds and bodies.
More than mere technique
dreams speak in images
that are as obstinate
as they are strange
more dramatic than logic
thought is linear
dream's holistic
direct and yet oblique
as foreign films.
When it speaks
we are reminded
language is wakefulness
dubbed onto our actions,
as crude, simplistic
as white subtitles
amidst the colour.
When it's over

it's what you saw
that you remember.

It seems the dying
take notice of their dreams
whereas the living
do more controlling
one is wisdom
one is ulterior motive
both are thrilling.
Dreams have common
subjects, like his
and her illicit skins
bodies caught in images
each is electric
murdering or at peace.
Even an old boot if dreamt
is Chekhov's gun upon the wall.
Go to sleep exhausted
you can wake up drained
two lives a day.
It's every part of us
Tao, wheel, rose, cross,
every pagan urging too.
Dreams save us from
the world the world
saves us from our dreams.

Climbing the Stairs

A man and a woman waver in and out of image, their voices and their footsteps intermittent. It is a strange experiment: to materialise at all, to meet and speak within each other's world is barely possible — each meeting of their minds must complement. It happens, after practice. It is the new world after all.

He needs them like writers need readers. He is a writer. He leans over his balcony, still calling as they quite separately walk past: 'Come on up,' he says, 'and check my world view.' They stare back, solid now, intent to find a text. And now they're part of it. Bring forward the invented to verify the invention.

She is blonde, so like Monroe, she pulls in the hand-rail like a rope but the climb exhausts the man behind her, too thin in his brown suit and puffing from exertion not from his pipe. His cheeks are gaunt, a day unshaven. Miller? Sartre??

What they don't tread on stays outside of recognition. It does not exist. Their parts must slip into their minds as simply as two visitors ascending. It is Monroe. Because the mind can choose but seems afraid to. She's chosen to be sane and put off ageing, so the paranoia's gone along with the wrinkles and the slewing of her buttocks.

There is no antidote to beauty and she lived among pharmacists. This drug they gave us, giving her: that which was 'dumb' but living imagery, was not dumb imagery: the blond hair, the red lips, the eyebrows, the full, low breasts, skirt billowing above those legs all that skin-touch down into the fierce, concentrated heels.

So now she's sane and we are dumb. She's climbing up these adoring stares that disappear as each foot is lifted like water drawing back beneath the waves. This is what was built on the other side of beauty: this woman climbing on and on.

2

She's dead now but she climbs the stairs.
The long legs that have gone
climb the stairs.
                    On a wall of a corner shop
the updraft of air makes her white dress
the parachute no one packed for her.
She has thrown off the penetrating father,
stared hard at the men rowed behind him.
Is the love of a woman enough for her?

Still, she is climbing the stairs,
each step as bare as a tablet.

The man she must attract like a Mata Hari
is just as deadly, when in grief or
in shallowness, incomprehension, can't
give the strange secret of recognition,
or none she can recognise, or fall on.

The blond hair and the body have gone
but still there she climbs the stairs.

If we think best, feel best
by seeing, so her body we are seeing
isn't there? Not at all dumb imagery,
she speaks as we all speak,
from our skins.
                    She will stay in the sky
pouting down at us, her breasts cool
or wound up like spinning tops, or soft
and yeasty as a freshly baked loaf.
Fully clothed, she is barest,
her red lips saying and her mesh stockings
sown with this lacework of Ohs.

When the writing is on her, even this
won't pull her back, just like
those best placed young Catholics
who slept with her, and the doctors

whose ministrations were
narcotic as confessionals,
did not.

She is sane now and beautiful.
She will stay in the sky when we leave it,
climbing her stairs.

Final Dreams

You drank strange wines; they were
your self, disordered, the character
rising from its own lees. You dream now
of her or him or simply to return to land.
Each memory a nerve-point on meridians.

They are your own but they are set down
on latitude and longitude, they are then
the world's. You are the world down small,
the gap between fact and imagery remains.

Working on what you see – the navigation
through wind-shifts – waves drive at you
like a greater set of truths
that won't be won by dreams, as they won't

by drugs. These are the same island
made fabulous or terrible
by excess. Someone must be awake
to see the ironies, to steer in such romance.

You make other waves between them
coming home to accident, coming home
to time and routines and the sudden
back-end of dramas you'd not perceived.

The chairs that press onto slate at home
press through you to the bone
press through the metre-long column
of the spine, lift into the continent of brain
the way your hand falls to the wine glass.

The mysteries remain. They are what you desire.
The polished apple a second away from your teeth.
You would see it whole even as you eat.
And yet it will be gone.

Return from the Sky

Gradually from the ground up — the city becomes real.
The nib-pen lines of architects' and engineers' ink,
water mixed with grey cement and inside, links
vertical and horizontal — meridians and their needles
of reinforcing steel. All this one
scratch away from swamp (and sometimes through)
where the many-coloured powders settle:
the greys, the ambers, the ochres, the pinks.
Old stones take morphology from air
and climb vertically, face-up with glass.
Beneath feet that are not yet there
streets expose slowly, and milky at first, polaroids
of legs walking, rising into trunks, arms heads.
The shortest have sight first, suffer the world
growing up. Children take the biggest shock.

Hundred-year-old gums and puny seedlings
gather at once, lawns jump and stop. Walls collect
in houses. On the ground, on floors, people rest,
are derelict, or having sex, appearing suddenly.
A window cleaner's cage, the bucket the sponge
then the cleaner. A lift descends from nowhere
with a body on a trolley, face covered by a sheet.
Birds appear in the air, on poles, power-lines,
young trees have grown, the oldest on their way.
The city is poured into its form: a person stands
near an edge, machines drumming, ducts seem
to deliver three women in bikinis near a pool.

Here and there a pause in the intermittent rising
as men go off the job, put down the instruments
and the plans they had spread like astrology
for a union meeting several floors below
and several minutes earlier.
                              The lift-well has grown
a square and empty tower with cables for spine.
A resuscitation machine is wheeled to a corner
as the doctors shake their head. The lift light

is approaching bottom floor.
                              Some celebrity
appears in his penthouse, uppermost if not crust,
wealthy as the modern gods are.
                              The fire equipment
reddens and waits. The city is back again, intact.
And there – one thin trail of smoke above it
like a line of ink.
The whole city is suspended from it.

The Well Mouth

Prologue

The isle is full of noises,
Sounds, and sweet airs that give delight and hurt not.
Sometimes a thousand twangling instruments
Will hum about mine ears, and sometime voices
That, if I then had waked after long sleep,
Will make me sleep again.

The Tempest — Act III, Scene ii, lines 147-152

Tiresias saw a pair of copulating snakes and struck them with his stick. This displeased Hera who punished Tiresias by transforming him into a woman. As a woman, Tiresias became a seer and according to some versions of the tale was a prostitute.

He fell on me dragged me from the car
already dead. Dropped me down a well
– and left. I am a ghost inside a bottle

If you look down if you put aside
parent-fear of wells collapsing how
the earth will fall upon you

If you lean over the heartbeat thud
of looking down you'll see me not as white
but black iron water like a fixed pupil

I see the bodies of the dead I hear them
speaking as they seek their harbour
I am alone among the heavy metals

The inlets are full of spawn and fish gasp on
the water's edge their gills like small accordions
opening into red the stories of the dead

You feel nothing in mud but mud's
darkness its walls hug all sound
until it stales. I feel the well-casing

body of broken things on me heartbeat
and breath come to me but consciously
by will: one breath one beat the lungs

need to be told: two three ... keep on.
Am I alive then? My head full of jags jug
the water brim-full of steel and boards.

My pale skin turning into burnished film
of mineral blue-green hallucinating water.
Its surface glows brittle as a sheet of mica.

Above me the well mouth one disc
of light an optic fibre white angelic
a creature its wings empty.

I scream and feel the scream lift
up the concrete liners into the blue flare
like a bullet whirled up by rifling.

I want to rise up in my scream
levitate inside it through the light
like a muezzin crying from a minaret.

But. What happens to the wasted if not
this thrown down a shaft and left for dead.
I am a dark pupil left in the meniscus.

I begin to drift on cool artesian streams
I pass underneath the spirits of the dead.

Have I chosen this have I emptied myself into
myself like mixing drinks between two glasses?

There at the pouring everything's at risk
of spilling nothing's quite a hundred proof.

And it's nothing to be hearing voices I cannot
always understand I cannot quite resist.

They flood over me onto my tongue
opening into red. The echoes of the dead.

Perhaps I steal them. Perhaps I am like Shiva
shuddering in his sleep. Again and again.

I am the luge I am spilling out of me from grave to sunshine on the water-
roads under coal and the nation's heatstink. yes I hear things never said. but in
the well mouth I can't change anything. change has gone.

Part 1

Rats. Too many of them in the ship's holds
gnashing on the grain when I moved in
        saw them scattering to the corners
like dull marbles
            shooting down corridors.
Dark minds saw them come back in words
vermin under the spring
clip of this file, in
the sharp teeth
of Helvetica
        But I could see them
        this idiot-savant that I am
could count them
like spilt sticks
my eye as fast for rats
as Rainman's.

The bosses couldn't see them:
He's the sort of guy who just wants
to shit in the palace
And container ships held in port
by my too literal vision
        went floating out
like Jarlsberg cheese.

When it happens again, it's drugs.
I might consider the general humour
theory: advantage, reciprocity,
to consider the detail differently,
find some way to see the surfaces but
miss the rest.

My doctor notes my skin the blotches
                are like beetroot
                and the Indonesian Islands.
And how like a counting device
my right knee clicks when I walk
how the nerves tremble down me

And the bosses and their mates and …

who else?
suggest a re-write:
that my ship comes in
when theirs goes out.

They know something that I do
not: yielding is macho
stubbornness is wet.

But I know
pedantry's a passion and no-one
understands the art of it, its cult of one,
its serious attention to the facts.

The metaphysics
of staying honest.

And two men
lean on my door looking
like the same joke I have seen
but never laughed at — and speak of
Tax Department Audit. *Whistleblower*

The doctor adds condition of my stomach:
like some kind of Gothic hall
rent with rain and lightning.
                              Police
inspect my car and in a flash I could almost
admire, find rats, and drugs.
The late-night telephone calls, three seconds ECT
                              then click.
I am written out of my health
with innocent, blameless prose.

*free to listen. good or bad I hear it. they are dead. they have only memory
and the worrying through of final things. vibrations in my water. I drift on
streams. my luge and the poem underneath this pain. I am* translating

Who am I when the cheque of me bounces?

When chemicals spill in holds or passageways
                    or in the stomach late at night
under the desk lamp: the second draft
of my dissertation on unfair dismissal
takes the skin clear off my writing hand,
my face.

            And how unshakably
                    it spreads,
seeing my wife and children leaving
my one-size-fits-all obsession, the awful
click in my knee as the front door closes.

Now I must for everything
see death hauled through the books.
Never thought they'd do this.

My face tight as dried varnish.
Underneath it I want to breathe in
lungfulls of air and crack my

chrysalis like a hear-ye cicada
into air that's clear, into sunlight
that is sun and light that is light.

his cargo his ship the ghost-ship one crazed man on board. the burden of
someone else's guilt turned onto him. ah yes. there was a crooked man I
knew and he had a crooked heart. I wanted to get from underneath it too

Where the bridge's south foundation rests
in dark suspicious mud, the Burnley tunnel's

stressing concrete to keep back, keep neutral,
things are buried, things lost from the world

of chance and sighting, of chance sighting,
are sunk. Soon – the carbon copy of my body.

Someone washing mud off their hands, the pug
stuck to the boots, how it stank and he would

never forget. Bodies buried, burnt. Our sunk
black coal. Never whistle. Honest in this worst

sense. Never sink a pot again (ironic sinking)
greet a mate or read, too closely, specifications.

Living and dead recall the smell. At the arse-end:
one looking up, one down. The buried, the burier.

Two bodies crushing down the same few images.

my skin looks like a sheet of tinfoil crushed up spread out again. rainbows
torn. is that me pissing in my own bed? are my lips still blue? hello sailor.
no I'm not the eyeful you're after. hello officer. still walking the streets a free
man instead of turning pale in prison? I can hear you so you must be safe.
in hell

In the basement on top of concrete.
In the basement under water.

Barbecued but dead by gunshot
then flooded under municipal water.

The lake of himself, sundered, cindered,
sinned and sinned against the leak

the whistleblower. Inside the police
lean and fat men watch each other.

Corridors once open in his body are slammed
shut door by door the metal locks shot.

Some men do well but some do better.
They wet lust and coloured powder.

Forgetting nothing and saying nothing
some men go better some do down the well.

Some men go down the basement but
down there they meet El Nino.

*the gang hear nothing. he could not feel in slow motion. he could not feel
their two bullets flying through him like birds. and now he's forgotten
it the memory of two shots is silence. is water creeping over itself ever
southwards as he moves northwards. is birds passing northwards as he is
moving southwards. he is a lean man not a fat man. he is going the wrong
way as always. I am the lake of him listening.*

Hers

One at a time men, subdued by spaces
they undress in, by the glass-sided shower
they must wash in (or I'll not touch them).
Men are not as clean as women some wipe
themselves badly. I am looking at them one
at a time ... he ... must walk through my air

that's heavier with ambiguity than he is
steaming from shower to the opened bed,
elephant, saris, those dirty Indian paintings
of bearded sex on horses, saddle-cocks
we call them. Naked women, kitschy men
and *his* cock like a small accordion.

At selection once three men stared at my
body up and down and one prick told me
turn around (like meat) bend, stretch, told
his friend: *have her.* Then stood there as he
had me. Well, it might have been worse.
Union: one behind and one in the mouth.

When a man's alone, sex's sleight of hand
will cock him in his body if not his mind
so he won't hurt me or anyone, all done
without him knowing. We talk but my
lips are sealed. He'll not get past them.
He'll get routine and it's not worth having.

My words tell men if my body's available
my eyes will them what the difference is.
My line of work shrinks their little brains.
The air between us heavy with elephants
the sex is static but time moves on and cum
ghosts against the condom.

this was my life. this was my life once. to wait outside the door for the
routine face onto deception. my face his face. doing up undoes again. chain-
smoking cigarettes chain-fucking men

His
Australian above the belt Brazilian below it
is how I like em. *Detective*, she says. Yeah. I am.

Never as smart as she looks on a screen,
trick-chic tanned by the sun-bed or spray-can.

Oh boy, this isn't a Turkish bath for copsikins
walloping women in towels to wind me up.

Her skin her eyes or lips, the old musk scent
smooths over worst where we look most

like the Sphinx's face shot by Napoleon's muskets
kiss me anyway (bitch) kiss me where I am

full of spunk where my hard-on makes you lisp
not the news report, the cameras, but collagen.

My skin is shot. Psoriasis acne the cancers
hooked on liquid nitrogen 2 square metres of skin

polyps and warts, and dry cross country
ambitious skin, skin is my tent in a desert

red as Polaroid snaps, red eye all-over skin
I want to be cognac-coloured not broken

capillaried, my shiraz, my sun-overheaded
overloaded, Scheherezading skin. Once …

Like those rough guys: not a Caravaggio not
Velasquez' beautiful black model (but then,

I'm no slave, not all day in the mirror, either)
ah, I'm as cruel as … I'm as fond of women ..?

don't ask them anything while they're looking. they can't see and speak at
the same time. they worry what they see spreads onto them. that the wife
can see it when he gets home. is my cunt still there in his eyes so she can see
it? this was my life.

Some are thrown off a cliff some are drowned
but mainly the gun It's safer you see them die

Why? Money like a newspaper cut down small
a stack or a phonebook the chunk-size of $100s

It's spreadsheets of the business and its profit
and loss figuring figures only I know which

No amateurs so pay right even so it's best done
yourself The visuals aren't as good as the movies

The blast in your hand opening in his face
blood's junk mate it's junk and a fucking mess

Air shivers between the notes Money is music
just missing that something you know is missing

Maybe only by thinking it might be there so
makes it obvious it isn't What? Fucking idiot

I'm a winner I don't have any medals for it like
a sport I've got something better The badge

bastard shot me in the left breast. shotgun. that's your tit gone he said. after
so many forced fucks to line his knickers with. But my tits lived on.

Having changed plans suddenly
head straight home from the game
a young girl and her father driving –
the first time he has ever stalled
on the built-up level of the railway
embankment and the sign empty
as the train hits them, nine minutes
thirty seven seconds late, exactly.

A diver near dead-white from stingrays
carried by freak currents and beached
onto a fenced-off untracked peninsula
visited just that hour that day of the year
by a doctor in a four-wheel drive with CB
who calls the helicopter paramedics ...
the ocean silver and breath like a bird.

In the faith-world there are bells
and boom gates that work every
time, the facts are like sleepers and
go right past to an empty terminus
and butt against the sunlit earth ...
Das lied von der Erde

Mahler sits down to write his
under-prayer *Die Kindertotenlieder*
and the near-dead slip away from
the music on the stands, he begins
finishing the story by starting it,
after his close friend turning manic
superstitious tries to stop him: how
dare he write the deaths of children
and still kiss them each at night.

And what awful music is composed
behind the shoulders, on unlit beaches
as the Mahlers' first child dies. God
invisible and empty, as always.

not fat tenors stiff sopranos but pinging bellbirds. they sound silver but are
vicious dun little birds among the whimbrels and godwits, pratincoles, snipe,
osprey the bi-polar birds

Nobody can explain
not like a movie loading on the apprehension
I don't know how with her so trusting beside me
invisible as navigation
I drive towards the railway crossing
like a peach falling to the floor

One car one line one train
wheat grown to head beside the track –
one world – or this infinity of stars
pulling steel onto steel
this child of ten beside me
living softly in a book not in her
body of a daughter

Geometry and gravity
this one day one car one blank
dayscreen uncaring in the universe
driving home and I am human-
blind inside my voices like
a man falling from a platform
or a wheelchair's castor jamming
in the gutter of the line

But stalling on the ramp? The rail
the sun peaceful as the bell birds'
laid back call the one lost alarm
as we hear nothing nothing
but the same recurring images
the one train approaching like
a peach towards the floor.

the rainbird. the pallid cuckoo. brush cuckoo. ecstatic and mordant their
ascending and falling scales. makes me cry to remember them. under the
poem the song as limpid as

She takes the brush and the bottle of silver
and as soon as she has painted them

her fingernails are wet and grow from her
like roads under a sunshower the cars

kissing through in showers of blue spray
at the patisserie the beautiful white dusting

on the cakes from her first mouthful
lifts her from the ground where she touches

against the office tower its glassy gold bullion
in the late afternoon, melting like Monet's

water into shadowy downstream, she hears
Sibelius' swans beating slowly into the air

her pulse beating, the child at the bus stop
so beautiful her skin more musical even

than music it is all feel and no finish
she hears it in the sky where there are no

clouds, before the sky bends down into
liquid on the glass the wings of five swans

the curve underneath the spray the soft brush
filling her body the silver colour touched

so carefully onto her nails, as in another
breath her lover tongues full onto her

and she ... and she ...

once she knows how to start to start to she starts to more often. moreofthem.
this one story no one else contains

Jesus, the ticker. I'm caught on the job.
Sixty-three, politician, ex businessman, ex

-everything, I'm still balanced on the her
of this hooker I've never seen, her black

suspender belt (I'm old-fashioned, I asked)
slung over her white thigh and my thumb

still in it as she tips me aside. I've got off
everything but this will stick just like my

condom. Gawd, there's a Van Gogh print
on the wall I cannot see beyond, his ear

wrapped, pipe in his mouth and cigarette
smoke all over me, the flat emptiness of

my socks, my poor old shoes, my poor
unthinking faithful shoes, the carpet's

vinaigrette. Her kisses held back: open lips
but teeth together, like kissing a fridge.

It's not love, it's itinerary. I wanted to come
fast twice or once slowly, but got confused.

and this was my life. I always feared a stiff. having feared much worse but
this is something I shudder over (having been under) many times before I
shudder less. he will make the news and every colleague will shiver at the
there but for the grace of God goes it. at least it wasn't underage. or the dog

Surfaces

Imagine it
there being none
to be inside everything
have only the mystics
inner waterfall
subcutaneous as heaven

Knowledge as a sudden pulse
if there is one
like music without the ear
or the spasm, that tiny deer,
without the touch
that startled it

Helen Keller listening
to Caruso singing
her fingertips
on his throat
the moth
the rain

Sometimes you sleep
and spirits visit you
like bales of light
there's no rush
or closure
the glow-worm

If I feel you as me
am I death's
analysand?
like something
revealed at the moment
when it isn't

If you were to dive in me
my cool aquifer
you would be
the one image in my eye
Tiresias seeing all
sees nothing

My prescience my salt
tablecloth
my being low in the water
like silt
our heavier intractable
Id

ventriloquist

A crash? The train? I am sitting everywhere but where
in us is that? Beside me a man is held together with thread
sewn through his arms and cheeks. His breath is full of holes.

One old black woman cries out for her son. Lost but no
don't say it. When a sweating swearing football team arrives,
I'm feeling lost. If they do, then we don't, belong in this.

Still on the train. So when a man tells me that a car
derailed us near a country town I start to feel sick.
He says the young girl and her father turned to ink.

Who was the man who told me? Along the aisle of No
comes Yes who knows where he comes from sits beside me
calling the girl to us, to come, and come to us she does.

Slowly, head in a book, here where no one reads.
A man sewn up. A son-less woman. Me. A dark-glassed
team of yobs crying now they realise they're dead.

And cause of it, this gentle man, the *father* of the quiet girl
who now looks up, no steel wreckage left, no train, no blood
just air, and ink. What's fair? What's just? Just us.

after luck or lack of. after dying or daying of. after nomorrow tomorrow of.
after all

She thought he wouldn't
have the weight of nerve
to turn steely drop
unhinged storeys
down onto the street
from openandshut shock
to this into onto he was
taken by the water time:
each nihilistic drop.

So he plunged she
was stunned and that he
caught the air clumsily at
first then one floor from
the painted lines seemed
to get it right, his body slim
as a plimsol from falling

extravagant big ideas a
sudden shadow like a bird
between the ballet mirrors
of modernist glass buildings
the *delicacy* of birds

not the shooting up
the talking therapy not
the zzappy clamps sizzling
him red as a sausage as

up from him flew his white
handkerchief its pathetic
metaphor

addiction is not real. it is a parallel universe. screens glow through my
fingernails whenever the voice. don't move. it will be all right. a principle
of curves, clouds, seductions. sometimes the late time of the day her skin
spray-on fuckable she liked to say she leant back and wondered if she
damned these young unstable men she drew to her

I rise, I darken the surface in damp hair
under ghost gums, blush pink and white
in Lake Eyre country, listening for your
last orders for your first dialogue for
the boatman the boatwoman the plunge
into valleys as silence flows above fresh
water like a single white crane

She has walked off the suburb into scrub, feels the heat
go the cold nights go hard against the houses.

It is death creeping back into the places it had left:
stones dislodged by sunlight, the sun's steel ball

one slow sweep a day knocking down the wall, and night,
the blue-green the bottle-sheen the insects of night …

(For every in-or-outdoor place
there is a void. The worry of it

eats her face like monosyllables: pots boil
for hours, the steam tells her she is sad, she will die.

Cold then. The house different and the same.
Each day looking out. Light burning like panes of glass.)

In the bush, her heart and skin are white, the leeches
seize on her like shiny commas, the ticks fasten her in stops.

They bleed her and she, wordless, punctuates herself.
Now it must be piercing (but she was then) she makes

herself the story of the poem no one should read:
her style is the sky choosing to be rock, or

water crusting up like honeycomb inside a limb.
If not for snakes she might slide under the mud

dream the long notes of the river, drunk as an instrument,
the vessel swashed over and over, the sad.

But we don't know. We don't have it said. If the sky cracks
into cold/front/blue like the lip of a cave swallowing her,

or rivers shit mud and cattle, or horses kick at snakes sideways
like dancers doing tap. The plunge of sunlight.

and now it comes to me. I am a glasshouse lit up at night. condensing in the cold

At night she cannot see herself. And she sleeps
blind for three nights. And she wakes as the purple song

pulls her mind open: each daypoint is a line, each breath
shakes a morning free of dishwash, the husband singing

like a ghostgum. The pain all over her is her own, the cold
is her own, the dirt's from the river not from shame.

And she doesn't feel she's made to die but now she *wants* to …
choosing it, the time, so soft inside her she could eat it,

so hard inside her she could batter stone with it.
She feels she's dead, down a well, read it and believes it

she is like the madam on the take but thrown down by
her crooked cop. You think she is there?

he will fall on his face soon enough when the gangs get it right and when
killing each other means killing him. let him tell them I am here first. tell
them that I know things

No nursery rhyme for the woodman of the district.
His face is black with dirt, hair like a doormat.
A visit to his woodyard is a haggling session
with a mad bull. *Hope you don't find anyone's*
fingers in the wood, you joke just once, then
count his seven fingers, one eye, one ravine.

The chip thuds like a dove into a window
of white, the saw-blade shivers then screams.
At first (or again): you live in your hands
resisting fear, each block hits the saw
like a war-zone, the shuddering the screams
until the wood parts. You relax, the blade
is stand-off, a muted howl as it breathes ...

Barefoot and bellied, face black,
he curses the jarrah bastard
woodblocks, the half-sawn.
His day is simple: everything
goes into the saw. And nights
in the shack with torn bags for
windows, TV, his 80 year old
Mum, sleeps in his day's dirt.
In ten more years he'll be coal.

He remembers
his father at the saw-bench:
a day full of saw-whine and
belt-slap, the constant
tick of the belt-joins, steel
pinched onto the leather lick
over pulleys like shrunken
train wheels

has not been seen since 2pm on Tuesday. police have been acting on
information given and the search parties have begun in the bush area near
the train line and the semi rural area east of. east of.

Wouldn't you know it, some bloke's been out
before the others and just to be sure,
he's taken a rifle, his rifle, the rifle.

He has known her as the nearly girl-
next-door, sort of pretty, sort of plain
(it makes some men see more)

enough to more than once, through
the window, want her, because, or if ...
he's a bit of a worry and she

she who doesn't play hard words across
her outline, her face/figure, she is ...
not at all what he thinks.

Out in the bush, her mind less,
her body more, her nakedness ...
But he won't guess she's made

love to the insects, her history,
her histamines, her blood. Staring up
from bites between her lips

they are painful lovers

*a cold light she might lie with their paralysis in her. on TV the face the face-
kissing microphone the newsy mouth frontstage as vaudeville and she is
made public. found and lost. the photo of her the missing woman the vexed
sign an overflashed Polaroid taken in tomato stew hardly possible to know.
ah yes. I know*

You sit there with a short black
waiting for the film to go in.
Tarantino. Wondering if he is some
beta-blocker ironist for guns.

I mean you don't take all the killing serious, don't be that uncool.
You don't believe that good/bad shit anymore, do you?

Foot massage, Ezekiel,
hamburgers to build the chill.
They're humorists and wits
these murderers. The heroin
makes John Travolta soft
as a wallet.

This is the world talking to itself?
Shooting up the distance
between subject and object
without a puncture mark?

[But

bang   bang   bang   bang

In a pizza house
in a lane
in a vehicle parked in a street
at a children's football game.]

shotguns handguns public places. his mate's wife's cousin's crim partner in
the shooting of the other lot whose contact was. fat ones skinny ones tattooed
and raddled ones all on the take on the laying it out. his brother's cousin's
crim man on the inside cop and drug man bag man whose wife represents
them. again and again

Behind the farm sheds' slab-sides from the 90s the 1890s
he used the rifles the shotgun but saw the Wild West
the steel-bodied Winchester he fired out in the bush,
its .45 calibre rammed back his shoulder and knocked
down rabbits like a hammer blow.

It's trendy. Silverware: guns.
Ain't life just a film, anyway,
down at the reservoir, dogs.
Blood saturates the man's front
so he wears the trendiest red silk
wit in workclothes (yes, a suit)
and yes, our wit's a slum.

Don't forget he's got a gun
as he d/l/ies there on the set
then yes, it's hi ho silver, and it is
irony he aims:

dove   dove   dove

'Hey, man! Don't shoot!' *dove*

[Each heartbeat beats
one third of a pint
back into the arteries.]

dove   dove   the words blow out the other side of him.
I can't remember   what they mean.
'Hey, man.'

                    dove   dove

*they did it to me. in their suits on the courthouse steps they. I want to break
their fucking necks shoot until it's blood and brains everywhere. just like
movies. but without the pissweak fucking jokes*

They come for the woodman in four cars
sirens screaming like the blade in wood.
He's no Arnie, Claude van Damme (once a dancer?)
he limps down as they rev up to him.

Killers don't wear suits, or wash,
they roar like Polyphemus from
the cave. He is dragged off yelling
to a station bleached by cameras.

Until his frail old mum, hair white as onion
climbed up into his smashed red truck
and roared into town to take him back.

Perhaps they sat and saw him on TV
that night, seeing nothing like apology
for, police had said, a mistake, acting
on information.

The sawblade swallows
air, hyperventilates,
the teeth disappear.

Still out there searching for the lost woman
into the ferns and undergrowth with
found today shallow grave   half naked
(we know which half) phrases
expected in the papers.

it is real enough to swear to. someone is visiting me and if there was
someone to swear to I would swear to them that. is it always someone
different. must be the figure I take in the figure who resists me. that was my
life. but now it is comforting

The ground are prickles. Some of her are lost, loves, peacefulness is
not people-love, not shine and sharp thigh-deep currents of the river,

nor are these words like the ground, the frost, the poetry lost from
the alphabet she breathed when she comes back, unfound,

wet, dry anger in her head, heart unmysticked,
walking naked but for a hair-shirt of ticks and lice.

She has no stories no explanation.
The sky crinkles like cellophane.

But she is wrapped in a blanket marked POLICE.
Pain sent her out and pain has brought her back

her period begun. When they see blood they scent her like sharks.
Cannot even darkly understand.

and me of all people. I think about disappearance a lot. waste little time on
what they say of it. news and more news and not a drop of sense in it. then
I have taken my time

Hello Mr Jones. How are you today?
Me? ... How would I know?
She shifts one foot back onto the stool:
Do you want your other foot up too?
He stares at his feet then looks at her:
How many more have I got?

(The general anaesthetic is a black nurse.
All the words fade when he looks at her.
Everything he tells her she forgets.
The bullets tore through his chest
and blew out the other side of him
like words, interrogations. He feels
the bandage like a shoulder-holster,
his life is held there, dangerous.)

(You wake and there are soldiers
in steelframe beds, the desert of Syria
under your eyelids. You walk in air.
In fifty years the mere carcinomas
heal like a strafe of bullet wounds
but one fraught visit from anaesthetic
and you fall down at home the black
parachute slumped over you.)

(And for months, like
practice jumps in horror
films: you plunge into the darkening
liftwell, everyone you've known is
crowding through. You say to her:
Just once, just once, I'd like to feel
the ground before I hit. But your neck
pounds, you hit the floor dreaming.)

unseen wounds. dark unphotogenic gunshots. a needle-threading lightness
gone the I gone with it.

(In the jungle, taunting, unseen,
the Japanese set up a wavering chant
hidden and wide, fifty metres in front
of the few Australians, and flanking
them on both sides. The Jap officer
in English: *That must frighten you.*
is shocked to hear them shout:
Ah, fuck off you bloody idiot.
You bastards couldn't sing if you tried.)

The Nursing Home blade is invisible
but the ceiling fan spins the air
down onto him, his worker's hands
long past work, and the sun whirrs
down the lino like a polisher.

The language of his house
was always clean: they did not do
the nouns and verbs which
dirty it. They were always
polishing and cleaning.

If you buck the end of a sentence
it throws the reader off onto
that other endless ground.
Death does it too. The mind
cannot carry the weight of it.

brave beyond our knowing. the few who lived but of them he said. how the
rabbits ran. how Blamey said it and they didn't shoot him. didn't. how one
soldier lifted his rifle and. but an officer gently pulled it down. no blame.
starving men their numbers dead beside them here for me to hear. no blame.
how they would all have done it if it could be done

118

His wife drew a lot when she was young.
Her sketchbook likenesses
of male and female faces

magazine and movie styles of then:
coats and hats, collars up like cowls
20s, 30s fashion, the lifted Dietrich

cheekbones and the long cigarette
accessory, the belted English raincoat.
Dementia wasn't in her Bible.

She sees a dried-out dracaena in a pot,
hears the lunatic canary on the side verandah,
the old woman who's become

a baritone: every day she's bellowing some song
like a deeper Florence Foster Jenkins
pain/and pain/killing.

To and from the same close-up, distant country
each day she waits beside him in a room
of women looking after pale men

their hand-to-hand combat with
the dying air.

behind the sheds were rusted cars cliffs of junk iron he bought at farm
auctions for a wink and a grin. they played with the chain. he lifted one
end and told his son to grab the other and then he'd heave all his power into
the chain up then down so the chain kicked like a bull in dirt. bucking and
writhing along the links until it hit the boy like a train. throwing him to the
ground

Her face wasn't sad. She left her hand
on my wrist and said as if to someone else:
death is not enough. There must be
love and death together. Or lack of love.

This strange integrity death insists on:
at your most intimate: as you are torn off the pad,
as your lines and life re-start before you,
I see it. Accept and release: no longer yours.

Ending is not your own, it only feels like it.
The loneliest minutes, saddest, most forsaken
are left out of us who go, have just gone
and do not know it. The mind living on.

The community ... no, the *intimacy* of death.
Your hand on my arm as you turn to whisper:
your car wasn't safe. You knew it, you blame
yourself. Your hand, the roll-over's

heavy crushing. Little coloured tablets
of light. No way of quite explaining bone
fracturing the pain playing like excruciating
music. I ladder like a stocking when I hear it.

Leave life as it lived you. SMS the gods. Do.
Your voice like an operatic shift: from pathos
to velocity, that trips my heart up. I am dead.
And yet you move me. No greater gift than that.

huh. my hero killed me. no little tablets with their more than sketchbook
likenesses their cartoons their gangly honeys and hopeless men. I leak tears
because he left me a double-entry deposit in the chest

Dragged me from the car
already dead.
Dropped me
down this disused
well disuse of me.
Fallen into disuse.
Or did it here (unlikely)
bashing or a shot?
Did he throw me
down alive to rot
slowly broken. Water
everywhere and
not   I can't remember

.

abject

.

The optic fibre!   white disc
angel in the well mouth
folding its wings and dropping
feet-first into the water
splashless (angel!) beside me.

My bones are disconnecting
the luxury of letting go.
I dissolve into the undercurrent
like a handful of water.

Artesia, Amnesia. The line breaking up

He must have tried to
(wouldn't you?) cover it
board over the well mouth.
Darkness. Now that I'm
dead I don't need light.

I will remember.

What do you remember?

Rockmelon. Wrapped in prosciutto.
Pulse in my wrist. Air on my face.
Faces…

Are you a man or a woman?

You must know —

.

subject

.

Disease.
Disuse.

Furs are gorgeous they fold
on my shoulders like sexual wings.
Men like it. The way it heightens
what they want beneath it
how it drapes on bare shoulders
slips down over my breasts.
They almost come just seeing it.

I am not a cupboard mink.
I fuck them with it. You pay and I

which subject is this?

Tell me who was dangerous?

Everyone.

Overhanging street light
well mouth at night

Blue wren
tail straight up
thin as a peg

bird calls the world's
pissing down with sound
rain in the bird

When you die?

when I die cover me with birds. when I die cover me with cats. cover me
with dogs. cover me with cows. I won't notice. but not men.

Remember her white hair the white
morning lying on the table is the only

clean and ironed thing inside the house.
A teenager dizzy after dancing

why and where who knows now,
but the floor like a shone shoe.

Her onion hair and skin, time like air
undressing a young man's body

in the old ghost standing at the door
the sound of air between his fingers

clicking like an abacus one by one
he worries at the endless the begun.

When her son walks through him
the air smells like boiling vegetables.

*

Their house worse than ever windows
covered with bags the smell strong.

He's been growing for thirty years
sawing wood until his unwashed face

is a forest. Neighbours hear them
but inside the rooms no love or hate

can answer whether they do or don't
in certain matters live as mother son.

*

A youth stands in his rented doorway:
What do you mean do I remember

hearing anything locally? She'd been
dead for weeks before he told anyone?

She woulda stuck to the floor… And then
his face turns white. *You mean she was*

Christ no so she and he was … in … my
fuckin bedroom. Yeah there's only one

all we never know. never. and it's a thousand times what we do or think we
do or hang our hang our head on. or over. hang on to. sometimes realise

No, not fantasies. Not repressed
memories, stepped-on dreams. Not that.
The opposite. Easy now.
Talk about
the last gasp
the straw that broke the camel's
if it kills me.

So be it. Those on the tip of the tongue
then gone   last impressions
count   I thought I had your dreams
but not   I have the last thoughts
last orders   last vengeance and lust
before you rattle and drop.

Bell birds
their tiny hammers pinging.
The ventilator
sucks.

I am underwater
but I hear through tubes of daylight
bell birds
pinging like sonar
the search ascending
from what is
submarine.

Part 2

My once-a-night cigarette blows like a ghost
behind me, wind is the pale arm on our shoulders

and the moon is full now like a white bowl
full of words read under the light: the page-

down encyclopedia of night. Because we talk
night into the thin numbers knowing only

being done with things gets the better of them,
salting the laugh, but playing the second-guess

is hardly dangerous and heady with it we
sew ourselves side by side into the future.

When the wind blows over us like a scarf
the night is an allusive tapestry of shadows

under the moon-glow. I slip onto him like
movement across a surface of water, he feels

the liquid kwarw-warble of magpies and my
shoulders swaying like upper branches

in the wind. We are poltergeists in reverse:
we are the future's ghosts.

not in one place I am everywhere at once. I am held together with water.
a swamp deep-set and paperbarked. I am where the river has lost its mind
in small ponds that reach under the ghost gums from the north west all the
way down to the city. Mansfield, to the cattle tracks the deep pissing streams
of the eastern tableland like diary writing

It's happening in bedrooms like another style,
slow anticipation, like someone rolling cigarettes

on the shape of it. There's a form of it in boardrooms
collectively, in studios. On advertising floors they plan

it past the possible, they make this echo-chamber
sounding like your own if you're a fool, to lead you

out of yours to this of no-one's. Taking the sucker
in colours and in nakedness like the satin model

you may buy of it, but must resist. Pornography
for those who find love hard. There are the shrunk-

sounds of those who wear the future up too close:
a V8 footdown from warble to scream

clearing a path inside the living, death as fast. Flames
rumpling their fierce silk when cynicism or despair

hurls up from the corrugated pages of a factory,
at 2am is writing arson, or somebody on fire.

This usual ghost, the past more truly dubbed
irresolution, like the crimp of petrol fumes in air.

Some find grass too green, the stairs still loose,
or boards carry the sound of pacing, adulterous

love-making, and the foot naked all the way up.
The wind at this life, the same unchangeable one.

*today I and yesterday when I said I I didn't realise. this I word this me that
is all sound and now given up to. that I am swimming in and away from.
an I losing or growing itself. flooding is so hard and so much easier to move
downstream*

They bring in a white bowl my beloved roast duck
succulent and crisp-skinned. It's Chinatown: they smoke,

read pig intestine menus. The air's full, the fish tank's
cardio-vascular, each side-lung heave of bubbles

the *feng shui* of things in place …

Except I want the flavour and the flavour's gone
all fishways. I chew on the memory of it, the skin.

Something else is grinding away in me like gears,
the heart of it, things turning but nothing happening.

All the flesh on hooks.

Then a mobile phone too bloody loud as always
starts up, a voice declaring less than half the sense:

Miss you Mum. Wish you were here. His words
are slow. *Wish you hadn't gone, Mum. Mum.*

Why am I hearing this? Why are the pauses long?

Her sad son. And the mum doing all the talking on
this lineage. I hear the son say it all again. I spoon

chilli oil onto the rice. He's gruff strine not executive
hormone, he keeps an open line. It can't be cheap.

I fiddle with my chopsticks, the food, the tea.

Miss you mum, wish you were here right now.
God, I want flavour but all I'm getting is story.

Guess he's a mother's boy. Look at my soggy choy sum.
A fish is lifted out of the tank. Then loud and clear

Since you went away Mum. Mum.

The flavour's gone. I turn sideways like a dying fish
and keep turning to look for him. Six tables behind.

By the mirror on the back wall. A big man with one
small cup of Chinese tea held to his lips. No phone.

for a moment I felt the room musty and old this man polished and old-
fashioned and cats everywhere and the only place to feel warm being in the
mind. that stove that steam. that watertank. those bubbles of oxygen. how
I'd like to push my face into them be engulfed by them my face in the side-
long heave of bubbles

Sixteen hours straight
the car like a boat loaded
to its gunnels with books the north-
eastern river flowing through the windscreen
                    I subtitle
with words pouring to the right
the flat rim of the long imagined journey
time and speed receive me on the set
car as vital accessory car as side-shot
tracking to soundtrack
the stationary car the travelling distance
bluemetal starway ahead under sunlight
the sun is filming the east then the north
                    then the west windows
of country towns I drive into like years
en-route to jobs
fearing the wheel-clamp the liver failure
country boys undoing everything in cars
dumb as cliché true under-foot
                    I drive in the breath
in front of dread in this ever leaving
passing underneath me artesian streams
lost years the love gone underground

Clouds fall like cliffs of air to both sides
the laksa-coloured soils after rain the grass
thinning into Nullarbor and the red-shift
                    soil with its mascot of eagles
standing on the verge in shaggy trousers
ripping at road-kill like old paratroopers
until I ask myself how a room
in the brain might keep this
the basket-thinning shrubs like ball-combs
or the flat-world famous for its naming
in Latin not the older languages of here and here
                    like forever paddocks
echoes of colony this politic this cutting out of corners
machines like symbols of the old men and women
                    totem and journey lines
I drive from one world to another.

The Yesterday junk is out
strangers who carried this world loose
beer cans fall from it and are left the road taken
                        not for them but death
greater than a traveler or the sum of travelers
even out here the Ampol guy says they chuck out stuff
they've been collecting in their cars for months
Dick bloody Smith brochures Myers sales in the bloody city
a lot of bloody use here
Love ya bird mate staring at the stuffed pheasant
I've balanced at head height in the passenger seat
a pheasant with no liquid in her eyes
but burnished red feathers on her breast
and a pool of gold sunlight sinks down her back
the burnished water on her skin
way below me where I dream

The sun sinking under the Plimsoll line of the desert
where straightness goads me
and open-ness empties me
out of one world into the next
dispiriting lines like courses through oceans
townships have formed just to have corners
distance immaculate the air like limestone
wearing down against the weather
night makes the road pale and the self thin
the cold aquarium green of the instruments

Driving as the sexual hunger of the eye
like a salmon fishes itself
upstream the eyes
bait for the lunging body
my eyes my arms up onto the wheel the endless steering
deeply wakeful for thousands of flat kilometres
pulling the future in like a lover

*my limestone internet my underwater artesianet my subcontinent. outages
pauses dropouts errors. they're the closest I get to living. I'm online. I'm the
lurker from hell. living in the briefest gaps. your disconnection*

(Opening before you like
Leonardo's thin anatomy drawings
of nerves ungenred the flat graphs
of 'fine art' a not-yet embryology
his child in the womb after he
had opened it to draw
heaven out of hell)
Stepping from the wreck …
unscathed, unexpected, upright
on both striding legs as if
from a room not a car-seat
wrenched off its runners
upside down, bolt-ends
gnashed by impact, as his
Hollywood in the phrasing
insouciance as always if
understating not playing out
boyo meets special effects.
Sunlight hammers the morning
into plates. Steel. You. You.
Perhaps a newish spotlight
burns the surface of the bonnet
better still the paddock
tray-like across the suns
everyday unceasing unstoppable
country, on this or that road.
Thin lines, anatomy, hell.
Maybe a sharp modernist
umph of buildings.
Even metaphysical waves
of epiphany, because he is,
and who wouldn't wish it,
able, after wreckage, to step
out through the dead light.

*the black water. a genius for making us fear the worst. the eye can't see
through opacities whether as Weismann's or Wittgenstein's conceptual
Barriers. ah. my bones are stepping out of the body. the past and the future
are at war*

What death starts
morticians finish.
Mortician or locksmith
he enters you he clunks
the soft tumblers
locked once and for all.

The sealed body.
What could be more
frightening
the shiny repulsion of a face
the stopped orifices
the poor old gutless
body.

Now that I can
I won't go back to watch
the funeral or the bird
swooping in to stall
wings alarming
over the coffin.

Who are they?
(Are the dead
in such a rush?
They forget
the living?)

*australia the words creep from our mouths like little scarab beetles as much
when we are alive as when we are dead. mouth full of turning away from.
nightbirds gnats. swallowing*

There are bees
fidgeting in the blossoms outside
I can count them
through the wall before the family
come then go again

I am looked after
months now so my feet are soft
what to say next
what is expected in each word
forgetting the track

Smell words buzzing
into my tongue more and more
she knows what
anyway what we've been through
but laugh about

Must be my children
they sit down and get up my jokes
this room is a replica
built inside the one I'm really in
bloody clever really

Must be who come
strangers pretending high heels
my son my daughters clack
clack leave me flowers its
who and who

I eat smells
I tell her my wife looks and just same
clothes hairdo now crying
black outlines her family
is a jawline

Just as dark dark
we always did you know late at dark
about who am I
eating icecream buzzing tongue
things flying the wall

Hurts heart
she breathes no heart green walls
green hair no
sleep no fire in the shop must put
out the bins heart

Sun the set broken
crack another red egg? yes what is
a honeymoon bees inside
the clock who are you tick tock
their little feet of honey

breasted and blind. they are hurt and humble but I hardly sound like
somebody from the Classics. no Prince for me. no toadstool but some toads.
none where I am going

She doesn't know she's three storeys tall
sitting cross-legged on a verge and playing
with the cars (funny stick figures in them)
in her one-after-babyhood white frock
and fat little legs. It's David Lynch Drive
until she smiles and old heaven swoons.
Parentless, orphaned by photography
which places her so hugely, bored, so
when people walk along the footpath
she picks them up and eats them as she
never ate her meals, never ate a thing
that wriggled. She sees the hospice just
next to her and naturally, because she
(think now, what image only promises
to the yet and the not yet … the icon …)
is curious, watching the elderly undoing
whatever was, a shirt, a blouse, a mind,
opened to the bone. She tips them over
and they die her death too. Like photos
she is dead. It might as well be true. It
might as well. This big child, her frock's
fine stitching, white as a camera flash.
She is Man Ray eating Max Dupain.

wind is so harsh it must be pushed by something, wrapping the world but coming in cold from the South. A gust of cold as if lifting the air from a miles deep drill-hole where it has been under everything, a less-than cubic metre of air, small as a child, a tiny bubble and a fur-seal under this net of ice or snare pressed flat as a flower in a book

Bricks and angels. Nothing to notice.
But the fish shop wall is painted blue.
How inside the wind there is silence.
Many have noted this but is there wind
inside that silence? Just the old binary
high, low pressure, the barometric
village. The man across the road walks
to the shops to cadge cigarettes and then
after smoking them, he eats. The cigarettes.
It's not disgusting if you're mad. He is.
Past the binary he takes in singularity.
God, imagine how his breath must stink.
I ask him, tell him not to, and he says:
Neither time nor sanity rolled their own.
Or Biblically: *Time stoppeth for no man.*
He's right, of course. Neither this I nor me,
nor me, I ... He swallows another cigarette.
He walks because of medication, I because
I must. I've been walking every day since ...
So we walk, past the single wall of bricks
painted blue so angels can pose against it.
Then a window-blind is flung up, its flash
bi-cameral, two cameras, so like the mind:
the fish shop is rank, grenadiers on special
their silver uniforms smothered in batter.
He laughs, his teeth jut loose – another butt,
don't break your mother's back on the crack
of pavements smeared with oil. Nothing
else. Angels? Not here. Wind. And silence.
Nothing special to note except the fish.
Every day filleted. Time is a fitness test.

now the water is calcified. I am drifting southwards hearing everything or.
another metre. thinking I am past intensity revenge sentimental hopes for love
and arh redemption

Something in the corner of her eye,
a chair as big as a small car
has crashed into the sideboard glass
and glass lies everywhere. The mute
jewelry of error, of accident
loose in the shoulders. Where she lies.
Not a public place, not cold bitumen
rash over her shoulders like a bloodied
stole. The loungeroom is everynight
but roadrage, his, of course, has struck
in the room, worse than her cerise
coat of paint on the side wall.
She sees everything in a clear 20/20
now best it's ever been and for what
her self/ above her dead/self 20/20.
Her step-self who came but never left
has escaped the past tense of her scene
only as police enter her private places.
It, everything, is. Don't touch anything.
They keep saying this too late now.
Not once in that past tense, confined,
he was, now, is, handcuffed, and taken
off, was/is first to leave the marriage.
She sees him in the backseat his spine
exposed, the nerve junctions pink and
white like pale switches all turned off.

then for once I want to be the man and screw her neck. mine. the woman
dumb enough to put up with him. to throttle the awful forgiving breath out
of her. to give in to self loathing and wrench her apart. I want to be the
animal I have locked up and prettied down failed in front of its red eyes
glaring all hell and poison if only it is requiem aeternam

Vision comes from heat-exchange
fear or insight from the side-wound
I see in circles a reflex of the one

giftedness I've ground one lens
of loss among the planks the iron my
hoops my ribs my blind body broken

I see the blue-flame dress of the sky
above me the small birds are angels
doxa polysemic words on white pages

the water has a heated-metal sheen
a film of whys and what-have-beens
is slicked over shoulders my breasts.

three kilometres from here it has
been raining: the water is rising
from below. ocean swell Hildegard's

migraine of God strobing up-brain
tunnel and birthing the down-up Id
death's other language. other poem.

a poem full of irony: the doubleness
of life / death. a presence where is isn't.
a poem is becoming pauses inside story.

poems written alive with the eyes closed
by poets fearful alert because they know
well a poem is death with its eyes open.

Night and the bombers are black speed
down through the under-sills of clouds.
We are behind them their urgent calm
formation, stately dark shapes in the dark.
Where? They are the black-pearled backs
of compound eyes under the dream sense
they are carrying from us nuclear and serious
not one image in formation argues less.

It's night and we're parachuting, we are
mushrooms with our roots trailing.
Each village silent, and each road left
night vision: in front of us as we pass
standing in a nightgown a dark woman
about to cross the road. Then all around
ball-gowned whirling on the dance floor
white satin, white suits, Viennese waltzing
white bombers in white under-sills of satin.

The bombers (back to black) keep on
through the war-film clouds, Dam Busters
perhaps, on and on, without the deafening
scream of engines, jet-whine (only clouds)
or drone. I'm up here behind them as
silent as the bombers, the escort jets
black buttoned up beside them, like suits.

And into this: some little bastard with a knife
stabs me. Steals ninety seven dollars, leaves
the cents, the cards, the mobile, and leaves
me in the bleeding loungeroom. The flies
landing in formation, the pathologist in white
gown the dark ambulance woman bending
over me, trolleying across the road of death.

at night. at night. at night. at night. at night. at night. at night. at night. at
night. at night.

142

In the paperbarks there were dead airmen in the trees
trussed like spiderkill in their beautiful chutes

Below the street the river-weed streamed bunching and waving
for returning soldiers – it was said you would drown in seconds

When the night paddocks were high-pitched with frog calls
I heard only the brilliant trickery of the stars

A boy said his little sister's thing was like a split pea
or was it the plump barley his mother poured into the soup

I smell the sap of fallen eucalypts – trees lying like stretchers
sun-sawn and sectioned firing volleys of light from their leaves

When I showed off my fart machine at home my father
stood and struck me in the face – not as funny as I'd thought

A war much closer than the stars and this slant and this
plump barley the possible mis-rememberings the peace

*the eye is poor research. it's too pragmatic. the skin is hysterical. it's too
much. or never enough. the weight of the past is in temporary storage. look
complex but keep your lips soft when you kiss. the foot is where imagination
starts. look after it.*

On a stretcher, on deck, on unspoken duty
to be dying, when the boat went over I was
launched on dark water without the boatman.

Inside, on a stretcher, in care, on duty
my temperature, my pale homunculus made
not a sound but waited for the call as cold

water stole out the heart of me. I floated,
the undrowned, the trussed-up, the face-up
floating lot of me, my leg shattered and my

feet bound – one twin of Clovis I held only
one car key that I might click and open hell
everywhere around me. As long as I did not

I'd stay alive. I held it and still hold it
but now I am dead. So trussed and still
I nearly lived. In the dark, in the too cold

to think but still enough to need, couldn't
help myself: I clicked it just to see, to feel
the warmth of its red light. And opened hell.

and never the key you want. the immobiliser. never the voice that says it all
and welcome back. there are voices. not the kind you really want

He is gangly not athletic: in the dark water
he wriggles like two eels in a pair of shorts.

She wants to love him and because she is water
and she knows what love feels like all over him

she knows what his skin is doing now underneath
so that he feels the way a river sidles up to a man

how the man has little to say in it but all the time
imagines he's Casanova not an eel or two in shorts.

I'm not the man I was, he thinks. I'd better lie down.
Why am I so wet and wriggling between her banks?

Where are my wife and my kids? But the water
kisses him and takes him off into a corner just

downstream. *I am something of an angel*, she says.
This is not seduction. Don't worry any more about

them. They have gone back. Above him the surface
is like a sheet of mica he will not see through again.

He will not see the sun. He will not see the moon.
There's nothing new to see when you are dead.

No disturbing anyone. *Remember they will be in pain,*
she tells him. *It's what the living mostly seem to live on.*

Whereas he is lying in end-music. He is its condition
its key and its fugues pull him apart its voices listen

for ecstasy not absolution. All angels are musicians.
In dark waters you can hear yourself adrift. Apart.

You are. You will hear no answers after the music.
Dark waters and dark... and the nothing that is dark.

or so light seems   when through the eye of a needle   a fish and an eel
and a stream

At fourteen
I try to be water

must climb off the ground seeking
soft lead from the flashings on rooves

in the furnace stir it into silver
liquid I watch all day like God

in bright shadows, having lead's
separate and merging properties

which blue over and are purpling
as a fresh bruise. Then I pour it

like mercury, into slow, cold blocks
I press into the pouches of the belt.

Then sink under the water, stay
like water in water as the waves

raise and lower me onto the reef.
Light enters the knowledge of water

and I live in it like an angel, I skim
afternoons like slowed down light.

But lungs are paper bags and air
makes me heavy, hurts me up into life

at fourteen saying *breathe*, wrestling me
at fourteen through the snorkel into light.

Cold upon the surface, still heaving,
every time under, then slowly rising,

the blood at the centre of my chest
a wheel the ocean seems to feed upon.

I hear it by middle ear, I hear *dive*
like lead, the molten and the blue.

Sinking.
Rising.

Part 3

At the pokies and maybe three vodkas
my little see-through boyfriends in glass.
Or maybe seeing the silly fruit fly past
in doubles or difference but never threes
hallucinated me, turned a wheel in my head
so I looked up and there he was beside
the screen on my right side – naked
as a good day in the mirror but hardly
Sean Connery this bloke, nice but, chubby,
it was his thing it was about a foot long
sticking straight up like I've never seen.
Don't know what came over me, I just
grabbed and pulled it down and three fruit
three golden pineapples clicked down.
I'm right handed, see, but suppose I wasn't.
This was a golden shower alright, not that
I let him go, just watched his jackpot
spurt into the tray in gleaming coins
my pipes and all shuddering like turning
on a tap too high then slamming it shut.
The world the wall the whole house moved
I can tell you. Then it was I saw his wings,
that he was an angel but a dirty one.
He had a vodka and I took him home.
He had insomnia, he stayed up all night.
I thought the roulette wheel was whizzing
and I was the ball, well, part of me was.
Next day I woke up with all the money
knew that he'd be gone. But he was there
smudged and sleepy. What a lever, what
combinations. He smelt of new coins but
he took the wrinkles out of my old notes.

he would, wouldn't he

Not her whole life flame-white in front of her
when she looks through the tunnel of light
and oxygen – installments lines in short

supply: blue lips red nails white expressions
people standing in the late light in the room.
Something more like doubt than delicacy

moves up through her skin her fingers
as she touches him takes him back his arms
bare skin moistening her chest that mantle

of air between their stomachs him face up
feeling the balance: of his buffeting thighs
of darkness and sweat between her fingers.

That she has been the first to forgive them
the old man in a white beard or the young
man with the cooler triangles of stubble.

After once too often as all the other times
lit her forgiveness like gas. One night
before her dinner her stomach thin with

argument the road not taken she just took
the road. And leaving him left him behind
full of ... something shuddering.

*they create loneliness around them. what they look at might make them
lonely but what they do afterwards doesn't help. what they do when they get
home. here they have paid to take their time and stare. they know their wives
or girlfriends would not be happy with. we hardly care.* requiem aeternam

After four years even water is forgetful:
but Lake Eyre is flooding with tributaries

converging through salt. Through wing
beats above the frequencies pelicans

are playing back the brine-shrimp
into beaks, their trawl-nets pale in freak

waters, the freak colours of salt.
This is the biggest colouring-in book.

El Nino is dreaming. It is drought, it is flood.
It is a lean man not a fat man.

It has no ear for music. And where it drifts
its imagery turns physical, by contrasts. shocks.

Out there, under the surface, a past life
swirls into a treble clef. Lake Eyre listens.

Lake Eyre receives music. It is an afterlife.
It hears water, birds whistling, the music.

*and below it under the salt under the pink and green surface. with an eye
this wide this open I see the universe. but that won't stop his sad face his low
impossible stories when they left him in a torched building. firemen and
flooding. all lives end with the story still running. I am going through a
painful transition. he went back and look where it got him.*

It's on TV, it's the only time you see me:
between stone pillars, on the courthouse steps,
in a suit again and my bodyguard a barrister
not a barrister, a QC (whining bastard).
You might well think that I was in a murder.

You're meant to. And watch me: I'm the Mob,
not bloody Caesar. I know a lot about him now
and how all the families shot each other.
After the top job? After the racket, mate.

Me? Shot some fuck in a pizza joint, tables
packed with dopey academics at Xmas lunch?
Me? Should have shot a few of them instead.
Except they love us, we're 'Mobsters', mate,
we're characters, we're the fucking Sopranos.

Put all the bent cops in a row and all you've got's
a gang of hooks for catching dough. Their word's
not worth a fuck. But I'm stuck here at the bloody
courthouse, walking on the stoney bloody steps.
What a cunt. Here's the only place that I exist.

so bloody stay there.
black space and black matter and a billion light years it comes to us and we
lift up our faces to it. is it anything but noise? the sound of the nerves

Thinking of only walking (the fluency of each leg)
to the Post Office, flat envelopes in the quiet box.

Cars turn his way and rev downhill into sunset
hit something invisible, a wall of nothing.

One car smashes ... then another ... five,
six. Then the unwieldy boxed delivery truck

stacked inwardly with frozen fish fingers, pulped
and crumbed, another car, a rampant V8 Rambo

rumble oomphed into silence and its sad steam
geysering up (the driver like a gashed fish).

As he walks they stack up back towards him
so he cannot cross the road because of them

he must get on and check his mail but they crash
into something utterly unseen, the good, the gross

spraying from underneath, hissing, crumples
which cannot rate themselves, or be let down

air-bags big bosomy mamas pressed onto them.
Something out there and something in his head.

Three months they'd told him, at first, then
second opinion. Less chance they assured him

than crossing the road and being crushed.
Each lymphocyte is strewn in front of him.

leukaemia. visiting the child the man the woman the lame the poor the fit
the unexpecting

I'm still down this
lost and found chute
no getting out of it
but items falling
down continuously
onto me my silicone
press their images
into me an imprint
a black hole

remember   me

Images to re-
constitute a final
moment come
to me to die
Is this perhaps
not a well at all
but a tower?

remember   me

From the opening
I might see on
the groundswell
way below me
trees branching
like bent type-
writer arms

but ah forget my fate

This woman, says the young woman
to the older woman, her mother
perhaps, *this woman likes to read
books about men doing awful things*

to women. Crime novels, horror then,
replies the older woman, the row
they're in, the bookshop of heaven
full of books from hell. *No, not*

fiction, assures the younger woman.
*She, this woman, wants to read what
really happens. What really happens?!
What men who do really have done*

*to women. She told me of a man
who cut them up and boiled up bits
then ate them. That kind of sick
stuff, it made me want to vomit.*

Really, says the older woman, *boils
them? Yes,* says the daughter, *do you
think we can find a book that
shows that kind of thing? Boils*

them? says the woman at the counter
to the women who ask of the woman
who reads what one man did or does
or men who really do do to women.

*clay sets around you its magnetic field bakes you a different dancer and it
takes you over points you somewhere north or south. your knee or cleavage
or hiplines orient to poles whether you like it or not. green parrots blue and
red-backed lorikeets clamour for you. the claque is gaudy but it's cheap. kick
up your valencies take the e-tabs and electrons*

Nothing special. The blades spin but you can't
see them. You cannot see the split-scenes of your death

They could be anywhere. Today it's near the sunset,
in the rain yesterday it was a slow thump of metal

Two cars shocked into silence the desolate language
of detail, absence. What they don't know keeps some

People superficial – the luck of the world, the shielding
close shave they walk away from – this is not to criticise

What could be worse than a public pool? a sudden choking,
the communal gut-retching chlorine, the emptying

Public end, not pissing in the water but empathy, the pumps.
To drown in the watery blades while they enjoy themselves

If you drown beneath it, in the subterranean under-currents
under words, finally, you will be underneath and wordless

Itself under water, Venice: some people travel into its light
just to drown, even in the shadows, of a noisy *pensione*

They afford it just this once: the slow-filling Freudian bath
above the water-womb, cutting themselves slowly loose

Or lower, in the churn of *vaporetti* blades above them,
hearing the sunset, hearing the hulls thud into the pier

have emptied myself into. myself. this. venetian masque plus daylight plus
darkness. bubbles. emptied. of air. behind the masque of drowning. I might
have had a thousand dopey sons by now. a thousand gorgeous daughters. the
seer has none. light spins in me like a tiny cyclone

But for her body never taken for granted
waking in its hive the workers' voices busy
at the day after a night's forgotten images
(what did we do?)

He felt lost and could not be found again
in nakedness between the sheets
Disappointment. Halitosis? Death?

For her *drunk* a relative term dealing with half glasses.
For him half dozens. He smokes in reduced fashion
(he can't stand saying *moderation*)
She has stood outside then noticing herself
the mirror her hands
splayed her posture
ludicrous and yet there's no denying *the Hindu lovers*

He is in love with glass. He loves its holding utterly to shape
by being see-through, liquid he loves for being contained.
She pulls up her skirt to show him a scar high on the leg
It looks like *semen smudged on her thigh*, he thinks…
He knows he shouldn't take it personally.
For seconds she is amazed by the one
and only unseen (walking with a stoop)
stranger there's nothing stranger than and

He thinks: *as we caress, I could live again in her cleavage*
the rear window is slipping with rain and nakedness
I cannot bear it.
Narcissus vs Resistance.
Unhappy with God's images of God.

aren't we all. are they even close.

It takes her in the face like an open hand.
Him in the hand like an open face.
Imagine nothing. Know she is honest on him
when he is not. Her best words in his
worst order? Sway-head, shoulders.

The lawn ran to grass and no sabre tooth
anything took care of it. No saving labour
emerged from his shoulders either winged
or unwinged, he was a layabout the papers
ran down in columns trained and sub-edited

for the same by the same few substances
cut here, cut there, words or blank cocaine
bank staff or colons. Periods. The conman
staff and viruses. Don't snort the stuff.
He tried but he preferred the horses.

Say when he left her he was winning
another horse race. One he had to hope
had a future not a pit in it. He unable
and she seeing it. Say she was left
but what a transom he stepped over.

Nothing prepares you for your life. Say.
Life is not aware of you. You are
of it, yes, preparing anyway, in case
for all the bastards in it, yes, but ..? Left.
Laugh. She was not nice either. Stayed.

Say, she had worn him out in argument
when he was arithmetic: which channel, ah,
which race. Not rave race another country.
She had gone to live there, slow to get it:
he had no breeding. She had no pace.
By a length, both lost. Neither bet on it.

onto the spinning floor. as I drift down-country. slowly as a dhow.
underneath you all

My thighs are wooden-armchair lean.
The scar? I did it easy, very wrong.
Knowing little is what makes us.
Room for more, most of it a pain.

Don't give me pills, leave the door shut.
It isn't diet keeping my body hard,
just mean-ness. I'm hard on carbohydrates
but harder on people. Take your top off.

Good. Firm. Ribs like shark gills,
your breasts tight, your lips thin.
We wouldn't last long in the Atlantic.

Sex is only collision. Two bony bodies,
a little bit of damage. That's honest.
Like a man's cock is always as fat
even if he isn't. A natural advantage
don't you think? Me on top, then you.

Go for it, go on, I'm paying you to.
Don't hold back on the sweat.
Ah the bang of protruding pelvises
the slurp of sex. You like my hands?

I could have been a vet. But I'm a cunt.
You too. Stay still while I lean over you.
Stop. I mean stop. I want to go in you
like this, eyes shut, like a cat being sick.

*

Then next day I'm on the sitwatch.
Sit in my car wishing it was Papal
armour-glass stuff in the windows
tap tap hard as trendy 80s oventops.
No bullets bursting in through that.

(Shoot the same spot, like the movies)
No one's dumb enough to stand that still
in real life, and believe me *they're dumb:*
sun on their black coats, black shades
heavy bloody shadows with outlines.

Sitting-surveillance, sitting like a plate.
My brain's photosensitive, I see everything
but who's watching me, then, eh? Me
the bloody cuckoo in the nest while he
is doing standover in the back room.

Here he comes. But I'm pulled down
the middle of my guts, my tongue's
grabbed from me. Shees, someone's got me
by the balls by the cock I'm I think I'm
bloody shot. Or it's my ulcer my heart my

my old red-back spider. No, he's got a
shotgun, he's coming back to ... Jesus, do
something before he gets in range. Before
the men in the cool-room take my mugshot
my face like a basin of uncooked mince.

this skinniest of taproots I reach above the waterline to pull it. bell rope.
him jangling on and on. the idiot. the idiot. the murderous poisonous
fucking dumb-rope of him. the light

Can the evil-looking cat with piss-coloured eyes
beat a cold-blooded lizard with dead eyes?

The cat and the lizard. Read that: the people smuggler
and the politician both of them rhymed with blood.

But only metaphorically: to be blooded have blood on
the hands be cold blooded bloodless have bad blood.

Ectomorphic choleric echolalaic these two boat men
on the Media Ocean bilious and overboarded repeating.

Until the dead eyes and piss-coloured eyes are one
the smuggler and the smug are both heartless unblood.

The women the children leaving a tyrant are the tyrant come.
Their safety and danger their innocence and guilt are one.

The rocket launcher and the rocket the gunship and the flame
of a child the dead-eye and the dead-eyed are one.

One for pity and one for having none. Piss in place of blood
the politician fawning to the racist and pitiless in the sun.

true or false that he won't get away with it. that he was said to be a man of
god before the boats. untested then the boss said. be hard on them. a hard
man must die first to be hard. look into his eyes. they are. he has

The song is now silent the rain cannot be seen
both are re-ordering the atoms lifting the brain

The ghazal has two leashes its two chromosomes
its two lips are sewn to and whisper two passions

To migrate to stay alive two long immigrations
above the surface and below again two voices

This song of two lovers two staves of sweet aria
move higher that thought or thinking of danger

Ghazals act without reason let the stern minister
lose his dead eye and his dead pulsing parent

His scales barely rustle. He is still then
he strikes. He is two. He is up when he's down

Let his dead eyes know he's the worst of men
his scales of poison. His cold administrations

Down where a voice lifts a head above your head
Eeyore be merciful. Mercy floats. Mercy lets in

someone has to fight. but how I want to give up. just give myself to
streaming sound. download me now. what am I talking about. you did. I lost
a hundred chances. some get there find the head loose and the heart open.
where he had been there is nothing

I'm deceased! I'm fucking dead. They'll never find her now.
No more. We have ways of making you talk — not now
you haven't. I'm a nasty bastard and that's for sure
and no sweet bellies no cops with halitosis
(the fags) will get down here and live to tell.
Underworld. You bet. I'm the blackest mussel
in the fucking river. Cook me, see my pretty orange tongue.
It's not saying anything. You've got nothing on me
dead or alive (as if) unless you find that fucking cow.
I didn't think of DNA. I never read *New Scientist*.
Nor my pretty face splashed across the 7 News.
But I wasn't on TV. I was on the take. Got it?

*finally. he tells me as if he cannot tell that I am her. things are never what
they seem. so he says there are rules within the rules and girls can't cheat
and only a goody-two-shoes reads them straight. two shoes is all they'll
find of the whistleblower. all his upstairs mates took care of him. he doesn't
want to know that he's been found. that he stinks and looks like mud. the
final take. and he's taken.* finito

Not one or two but nearly 100 cars dragged from the mud
with weeds like eels from the eyes and throat of a horse's head
mafia *Tin Drum*. The river police ... *the water rats, not the pigs*
(a local said) muttered never said what they found inside them.

You'd see the water spilling from their ladles and the slush
like sodden straw heads down searching for revelations:
a suitcase full of mudfish the greyest of grey soap in the boot.
Me! Wrists and ankles broken but curled up like a spare tyre.

100 cars! Fucking slowcoaches. My back cut by backseat coins
as in Everycar the handbrakes off as they leapt to their deaths.
Holdens more suicidal than most. Their big flanks ... You just
can't tell: always thought the anxious ones were the Fords.

And one that had drifted all the way from the other bank
underwater like an old bull slouching back to the herd.

finito *and then it will be too late so piles of crap on him from me. the way*
these slimes cross the duty into interest has to be seen to be believed. they
will start killing us all. they will kill each other as soon as the bosses get
onto it. their pride falling like gobs of semen

'She would have been of good woman,' the Misfit said, 'if it had been somebody there to shoot her every minute of her life.'

Flannery O' Connor, *A Good Man is Hard to Find*

I would have been a better man if there had been
no missus there to chew me every minute of my life

If there'd been no woman there to snuffle up to
to wipe my plate of misfits to snap me out of me

We blokey blokes think we are unique can't see
it was ever thus: *been somebody there before us.*

As lovers: if we are a ladies man to a ladies man
we might just be a ladies man to a homosexual

My brain is an idea I had to have but sometimes
my brain is more like porridge it makes me gag

What happens there is like the box of weevils:
chew everything. A good thought is hard to find

One pale thing wriggles hard behind another
thut that thut that thut that they congregate

Head-end to bum-end for and then backwards
to a standstill. There is the stopped sense of it

Empty paddocks. Creatures standing under trees.
The roadways cleared. The paddocks empty

A bird call flies from end to end of me

*underneath the country through the wild under-sponge of limestone my
body drifts on currents artesian and dreaming I am nearly there I can hear
the waves breaking up into my stream of being. my artesian dreams my
calling into myself the light of their forgetting*

I drift through the underwater
bodies of children washing past me in the flood
their world in red shift below the surface

a blouse ballooned with air
above. Not a Portuguese Man o' War
but a woman topless somewhere

drowned. The drowned in Asia's vast
Tsunami the drowned thousands washing
past me. Not in our wildest nightmare.

A single flower. A chair. A child.
Not a single flower or chair or child.
A hundred thousand like a war.

Where does disaster come from?
The billion tonnes of water the families
the waves lifting against the light

the families and debris
stunned fish in silhouette against the light.
No more. Please. No more.

the how of life from death. afterlives. our heart is born and dies broken.
the deluge and the cresting waves the water sirens are calling. I am nearly
home

Against prefabricated walls short of kind the world's
discerning conscience Yes or No asylum seekers do
not think of life and death as we might think of wine.

Your emails are sent to friends in big America.
Bush will be endorsing things you can't imagine.
Will Kissinger be indicted? Will they ever sign?

Her car was only six weeks old when the wild oats
next door drove right into her. Drunk to the end
of their towbars. Things are local. Primary votes.

George Bush? The present: one voice part pulled out
like a testicle. Kate Bush. Memories of homeland.
Bees in flowers are innocent. But we're in doubt.

Why should music make me cry as if I'd witnessed
everything? People came up close and now are dying.
By 'everything' I mean nothing. We are released?

The hole in Zen no one wants to talk about.

spilling into the ocean from my seepage stream my underground and
dreamy oxygen

burnt out treescape   these broken crotchets
only then
driving through the ruins   one vehicle's
soft tyremarks pressing in continuous lines
the ash
they notice   where the scrub has simply
disappeared in fire   left a stark opening
the black
well mouth

for Meredith

Alterworld

The living are already dead
—Krishna

Sologram

No sight. No matter. No repertoire of images
yet. Somewhere in my brain there is a hand.
No, not a loose hand waving or punching.
It's as real as television rating as Reality.
The body and its parts in me, in you,
within all of us this generic person
as sologram? The ransom: live my life for me
or I will waste away. Unless.
That is the agreement.
The world expands your heart and your heart
fills the world
like weather.

Despite the evidence you imagine
nothing has been in the world
before it arrives.
It arrives.
It alters.

In the Alterworld the Windows Are Open

The windows are open: and sounds are falling coldly
onto the world's floor, gravity is un-speaking them.
I am their poor translation
I am their immigration.
My heart burns.

The sounds keep shuffling in me, like pairs of old shoes,
mine or someone's, or cast-offs from the dead.
Then information enters me from five
directions. The senses. I hear endless
deserts and distress.

Objects. Ah, the innocence. Presents, rings, and jewels,
stainless steel appliances someone couldn't part with
from kitchens, a strainer, a touch-to-the-skin knife,
his glossy as river mussels five-year wok.
Her favourite recipes!

Then a body arrives, my sight slings over it and turns
it around again like a happy dog, I am inventing it
with all the turns of the world for sex, for myth …
All the time in the world is never enough.
Objects. Fixed opinions, the want.

Even his / her body beautiful, the turning, staring body
wrapped onto their generic body like cryovac,
with real tears for archetypal hopes. The lasers
outside it might be cold and wet and clear
singing ships onto the rocks.

Dusk comes, its green-tea light. And the black
wave of darkness enters me, its weather
passing across the sill and transom
like fainting without falling,
gone back into itself.

Their names and our history. Naming is neat and not wrong
but objects don't answer their names, they don't love back.
They are subversive. They have no conscience.
They are foreigners to us all but enter us.
Name me. They are amoral.

But thank God the bodies of the dead don't come back
thump onto the floor under the sill and say nothing
but want it said. Bodies. Corpses. A father's, dead
in the awe death does to us, cool breezes
arriving. The names compressing.

This ashtray was a highly machined 88mm German shell.
In summer it burnt in Normandy, and in winter ...
Russia. My hands holding a ... history haiku.
Range: 15 kilometres.
Target: Allied tanks.

The world keeps arriving through the windows.
Range 1: is five seconds less
than the length of your life.
Range 2: the length of your life
exactly.

Seeing the Pataphor

for Judith Crispin

I am slow this morning this morning
is so slow if I want it to be
I must work past its slowness

and as much falls through as fills
the holes and our job is to note
the difference

so hours don't pass they are not nutrients
in my brain the hours telling me
I am as blind as mushrooms

but see across the road this morning a man
stands on his garden path and a black
plastic bag barks and flaps beside him

at night in the wet that black bag lies flat
seeing the dark like a bat in the trees
the street lights are raining

We Called it the Engine

Nightly like a deeper and steelier sun the diesel
cranked over then thumped out its metal songs
of electricity, 32 volts in the darkroom batteries.

This otherness for darkness, its steady beating
on farms beyond the powerlines, a slow gunnery
on cold nights, a standing rhythm in summers.

You held the crank-handle and heaved it with
a bunned hand: thumb held aside so the diesel's
chance back-firing wouldn't break your thumb.

Stopping it was worse: reaching past the heavy
-spinning flywheel to the governor's lever, pushing
bare fingers against bull-steel massiveness, pushing

till it died. If you let go too soon the black heartbeat
re-started flanking over as it pushed back, resisted
your thin skin your small bones your fear.

The Red Route

for Miska G

Tyre-prints tracking through deep snow
pull the bus invisibly forward onto the dark route beyond
the trees half-wrapped in the sky's
white imagination.
From some angles the red bus must be red, but above the bus
the long lawn of snow on its roof
swallows bus into field. A white stop in the route behind.
The red bus is two-dimensional, entering, it glides sideways
like Robert Wilson stage-craft,
by this mime and tableau the timeless replacing itself as itself.

From this stop a woman steps down
warm and scarved and untouched: just herself, not a schema
of white, not walking off slowly
rumpled by everywhere the same. As the bus departs, its red
receding from her brown coat
and repelling the separation across this cold television
of time: other forces seem non-
existent and non-malignant where the whiteness
speaks and is white light, and enters
hard and as sunless as the inside of crevasses.
No thing likes or dislikes the old woman shuffling
with her snow-bag over her shoulder.

Snow is neutral, impossible becoming,
inside her thoughts of warmth, jumbles of words, the shopping list.
Becoming is unstoppable, mysterious, neutral as air
when even the advertising boards are slurring
and dishevelled as Bing Crosby in White Christmas
playing slow as the power runs down...
Snow-death, lights out, over time and space, entropied,
faux intrepid, a Christmassy
mould is extending, endlessly, over the tree claws
and outstations, its teeth
off-white and its gullets dark: the other-animals of snow.

Inside the bus. Each muffled figure is
becoming's slow cause and effect, breathe, blink, through us
like bad jokes heard under snow
unable to ignore this everywhere immensity of winter, soft
as white doorways into death.
Who is this old woman?
Now you have woken here from another world and into this
blanket of white echoes:
what you're seeing has seeped in from where you began.
Along the red route.

The Man with a Shattered World

for Alex Main

A palimpsest on the story of Zasetsky, brain-damaged in WWII, and his attempts to recover from chronic aphasia, observed by his physician A. R. Luria, the Russian neurologist.

Face-down in Id
shellshock
mudwound
generalanaesthesia
patronymic dreamsof
sexanddeath

as they lift you from   your ditch of star-shells
your eyes a crocodile's   opening from the mud

the light is migraine   the world is flat where
your name was   clouds of smudge

when you lift your head   from the pillow
the hospital glare   overwhelming overlit

as heaven the wards   crowded with the risen
stanza by stanza   mud into mudlight

* * * *

Ah, Zasetsky, they say, awake at last.
Faces and surgical corridors inside the eyes
stunned   that you must mime
someone who   mimes ?   in the space
left by   ?   Somewhere in your stomach
so urgent it makes you restless
down into the hole of you   you need to   ?
no what is it ? even for a   or for the
bedpan?

On Wednesday you try for hours   can't guess which day comes
after   or before   alternative words   nibble from your palm like
friendly birds   but what does 'after' mean?

If an elephant is big a fly is small   is an elephant bigger than a fly?
And try for hours   the pain pours up your spine   into your head
Does   it mean the elephant is
very small?

* * * *

Being shot in his left temporal parietal lobes
ruined his right side of everything — a cat-like pupil
pounds like a splinter in his brain:

the images a needle in a groove
should play back   crooning
its love of the world but his universe
recedes by half of everything
and half of every half is infinity
like a metaphysical conundrum

as the tilting halves of the township
are watching the women at home   The physicians leaning forwards
are watching   he stands nakedly before them:
he sees half of a head of cabbage   Rembrandt's *The Anatomy Lesson*
on the table in front of him, a leaf   and the colours of seriousness
then half of that leaf then   above dissection of the corpse.
half a crease...   He is some kind of *criminal?*

Pedagogues, scientists, reductionists,
he is halved: his own sight
sections everything
     (the physicians are)
     (sicians a)
     (cia)
     (i)

* * * *

He scrapes a journal
one at a time each letter
grey as a pigeon

trying to remember the word
before it / after it
a sentence lies there
like a street he starts
out knowing and
reaches the end of lost.

Language is in there
ancient as mineral.
He is new an angel
struck blind stutter

-ing each letter down
like a drill-head into
God.

* * * *

Where are the sentences of German, English, the moves from chess?
Where is *he*?
'Then I went to the front, it was terrible and cold, the flares, firing…
the German 88 mm shells tore tanks to shreds… ' The neighbour
was here yesterday then
he was gone. There is no meat in the butcher shops but butchers
stand there   people are queueing. On the farm   the worker who
gave him eggs, gone. 'What can it mean?
I am stupid!' What is happening?   no-one says.
('It must be my injury').

* * * *

Zasetsky hunches in the corner at home
stuttering, jolting and undone, as the years come,

his mother baking bread, crying into the dough, his sister not even
glancing at him as she leaves, and the visitors who pass by him
dropped like an old coat onto the chair.

Even with his eyes shut he is split: the right side swarms like hornets.
His face is the shadow he shaves each morning into cuts…
The razor is dog-legged, his face is cubist.

He cuts where he is not
he misses where he is.
His face soft metal.

* * * *

Wear your clothes neatly, keep your elbows
close to your sides, people won't think you're a lunatic
the sun landing in your head.

Then winter   bares the branches
thin and wet   like splayed nibs
blackened by ink   Cyrillic
pitching in the wind   and the word-nest
the harsh white   the river of him   the lake of ice.

I have lost my arms and legs! I can't find them!
Even the stars are different (a line of tracer-shot flies towards him
like asterisks) The stars are like miniatures in ice   but
miniatures of what? The stars gulp up abstraction, burn like
the dot to dot drawings in his brain.

My mother is an old woman covered in web! Professor Luria studies
his journal like a lecturer: What does this word "web" mean?
I … don't …

* * * *

He grips the pencil
like an etching tool
scores the surface
deeply each letter
goes down up into
the blind-sheet of his
left brain, the dark.
Cyrillics' bent rake.
Every day he forgets.
And starts again.

Who could blame him
falling down drunk in the street
the words burning his stomach

in farmyard fury, trapped, each
hobble and joint pain
a wrecked syntax.
For twenty five years
words give him back then strip him:
he stares at the pixelating
blackboard.

* * * *

If he has a lover, if,
then just to see her he must scan
back and forth as if shaking his head.
He stares through the window at cars.
He is a cat, the pupil's black line.
There's truth to conjugate: If an elephant is
bigger than a tank, is a 20 year old soldier... ?

Perhaps they took my brain out
altogether. Or cut the left side off
and put it back again. I dream.
I imagine with my right. I am
    a little brain left
    out in the snow.

    At night the air is cold
across the valley, a diesel
beats like a slow repeating gun.
Under the stars.
Looking up I can
taste the tang of constants
the black roof of my brain
scattered with salt.
The sky as heavy
as language.
And its smallest
black hole
a syllable
beating
i

Enfolding

There is a world inside this world.
Like someone's cigarette smoke
moves away from you, then over you.
It is fickle, it thins out past you.
This other world where things alter.
It can be beautiful. It can be musical.
It might burst out through your chest
and change everything forever.
But part of it resists you, un-hearing.
No? Or surfaces assume first place
like narcissists: you see only them.
You can't press a name onto them
like a stamp onto an envelope.
Addresses are not what they seem.
There is a cold, pure light outside.
You move out into it, naked as a car.
The alterworld will part, enfolding.

Tram Touch

Wanting to feel more ... than see too much:
long fingers stroking his jaw line, the sizzle
a day's growth makes.
She is listening, her thoughts her pataphor.
A kid is shuffling and jabbing at an e-game
palm up face down, like a small swimming.
Outside it is raining. No sound of it.
Easy to forget they are moving, her standing
weight to her feet as loneliness is to her soul
(her word for it, the sense and the place
she is and most heavily is not herself).
No sound of it. He sees her
as his hand moves to his throat unlike a man,
she thinks, he thinks, both, hand, and throat.
Whether it means, may not mean,
shared touch. Her mother would often when
embarrassed do this, or being phony, fake,
wrist bent forward and up where his is flat,
as if he's pulling off a cobweb, or the mask
a man, a women, arranges.
When she looks into his arms she sees waiting.
And later, biography. When people meet
it's always talk, talk. Here: withheld.
Nothing is as it seems but is as itself seeming
always more.
She breathes out, the doors open, night
enters wetly on the coats and the hair as
passengers step between them,
the stops.

The Architects of Ist and Dost

They turn left turn right the two of them disagree
through sentences like endless streets, they disagree
as verb – they disagree themselves, are dialogically

at odds… Mid sentence they run into Dostoyevsky
mad from moral questions, weapons in both pockets
casino chips scattered through his hair. This city,

he shouts. Why is this city? Now that virgins have
all gone and not to God but to bankers and chief
executive ruin. How can I write about this? Why

is money the biggest question after sin? Do my
words have to strip to pay their way, pole-dance,
gamble, plot and kill old widows before anyone

will take notice? The two architects have no time
for such things as fiction. Their concrete celebrities
their blue-glass-legged buildings stand in for them.

They struggle with power not moral action, they call
positive in the negative spaces, call their Dost into Ist
as solipsistic metaphysics, and cash-Gods of councils

are the nearest they feel to grace, and their drawings
rustle against planners, befuddling them with theory,
their Power-points drop clauses into contracts and

cartoons into cities. They hardly see the old novelist
shuffling for handouts beside them. He is shouting:
my buildings are in here (prods his head) and *there*

(pointing at them). Such buildings last centuries!
He faced a firing squad. They are dazzled by glass.
Dost wants to change all the money into words for

his old-fashioned God, they roll their fabulous dice
across tables and blueprints, taking home the cash.
Who wants to be as crazy as a Russian novelist?

The City of Ist and Dost

Natura naturata/Natura naturans (Spinoza)

The city squeals out a knubbled quarry of ice,
wrists of work, chains and trucks.
Yearning trams.
It is chopped out in a factory of coldrooms,
collected by darkness into brightness
and reassembled with tools of daylight
every daylight. Reassuring us
in Nothing, Something.
Chopping and squaring, lifting and stacking.
If Dost is verb, the city of Ist is catatonic.
Its eyes stand up on stalks.
Endless gratification.

When they under-sprayed the trees blue as ghosts
uplit along boulevardes invoking old Paris
it didn't work.
Tim Burton and garish faces, and Johnny Depp
not Paris. Cirque du Soleil, gaudy as pimps.
Blue as ice.
In the old stories ice is always about menace:
ice wants to get inside us,
then go dark.
Stationary in the cold, tourists, as their cameras
collect Ist, just now. In the ice, the static,
the noun of
layers, resting. Its Nothingness wants to get inside
us, then go dark.

The music. Hear it? Music is *and* moves, it gratifies:
music as Ist *and* Dost. Being noun and verb, music
is second-hand.
In us and of us. The substance direct.
Music is moving from somewhere else to rest
in us, then restless, on to somewhere else.
Next. The sound of Nothing. Ist.
Music is the metaphor cities make of architects.

Stillness, the cold, is real, it is in the air,
unlike snow
on black coats both sides of the Yarra bridges
girls dressed like frozen stars, the men
black holes.

The old arts of pleasure and lassitude, addiction
and silence.
The words of the poem are in front of you but
the poem is somewhere else.
No next and next, pleasure enters us like insight:
Ist is here from all heres, is the one thing,
like hope. Ist is of the blood, as blood
is of the poetry.
Dost is the task of Ist
in us.

Urban Streets Enigma

Not here it isn't.
When my shoulders turned left a few degrees ago, I was back
in a film, back to front in wars, sideways in the chorus line.

Boy, did I kick up my heels.
You do that. Yes? Frankly, there are times a turn of a phrase
out-dances me like Singin in the Snowstorm. Cold shoulder.

i.e. Out on the street again.
Morning fog glints on my suit, smatterings of Garamond font.
The cold front, the warm air rising ... I can't see further than

a two person thickness in front.
Inside me I consider my blood pressure, it is rising, my inner
barometric me, inner fogginess, incoming weather, or stroke.

I am that. I am inclement.
Perhaps I am stuck up my paradigm. Patadigm. She is standing in
the warm-th, warm-th... A personal crisis, that word. Pedestrian.

Then I say to myself:
you, are criticising me, for what you do all the time? A paradogma,
the box, the ticket, the phrase that makes em run. And your anger,

the genre (or genra) of itself.
Generations of cloning. And self-reflection is clinging, even
insisting. Oh, we are both wrong, you are as at fault as I am.

Just over-react more.
Cars squish through rain. I /me / anonymity. Systole and diastole.
Of my two-person thickness at a time. Rush. Rest. Resuscitation.

Enigmatic Beauty

Once I am inside the car in her own words
she is a long and dusty summer. The sun roof is a bright
blue Malevich always changing, always the same.
She drives like poetry, a flying creature, a question.

The seat belt is a tongue between her breasts
but not like you think it is, when it is you —
she is naked, it tongues her speech, her salty
insouciant skin, her hands around the wheel driving.
Speed her hunger, and question, this man-made beauty
nature alone can't give her, but like nature
a car is always naked, if anything is naked.
The word naked is naked but never as naked
as her car, her insouciance, pointing to the word.

At the corner she had stopped to pick up this man.
Her skin makes the man look at her. He sees about
and within her, shape and beauty, she is sexy but she
tells him she was once picked up by a man she
saw was a woman, she grew coppery wings
she argued like a hawk into these questions
beating and sexual and extraordinary.

I am a kind man, a man who stands on corners
of his own kind, I throw up the wrong signs,
never look manly, or naked, and at my raddled age
it's far too late to acquire the manly look
men have, not for a man who went from a boy
to a man and got lost in the soft between.
I am manly aching inside my unmanly skin.

But she goes through the gears like Lewis Hamilton.
She takes long corners like summer takes hot nights.
She says: beauty is soft and hard at the same time.
Its outline and inline are bewildering.
What is or isn't there to see moves us like speed.
Unmanly a man *looks* soft, but a woman who has no
womanly beauty looks hard or soft but never both.
The car, beautiful or ugly, is naked and hard. We drive
until the sunset rains. And the long yolk of summer
breaks over her, on the car, on me, on everything.

Urban Garden Enigma

Night is a black snail.

His mind is a battered four-wheel drive
he parks in their basement car park.
Dim fluorescent tubes lazy with ennui
are pastels and the colour of pellets.
A heavy door opens into the darkness.

Day is a lettuce.

Her mind is a series of built-in robes
she selects from knowing her clothes
the narratives she'll save her day with
are pastels and the colour of pellets.
The hours fall in her like lottery balls.

A snail. And a lettuce.

Here Come the Missionaries

Now when the bike-clip missionaries arrive
I turn them away fast. But for years
my head replayed their early visits to the farm:
they'd ridden miles of shocking gravel,
they had you by a sense of decency
to hear their hope, knowing endurance
seemed right in matters of belief.

Once, because I was alone perhaps,
I asked how mind could survive a span
of light years, say, how the Universe was
trillions times further out than Timothy Leary
yet a nucleus inside an atom stood
as we stood on the bustling kikuyu lawn
and electrons spun everywhere at once
in mother-of-pearl blur as far away as Africa.

It's in the Bible somewhere, one of them said,
fanning pages like someone counting notes
all fingerwork and that long *vrip* sound,
as they stood on a mat of fallen mulberries.
I told them of the span my father bridged
with three long stringers big as power-poles
dropped across the river, planked over
and joining both halves of the farm.

In the war the Public Works Department
burnt it down, then blankly ignored him
from their desks. As a returnee, penniless,
reduced by dengue fever and malaria,
floored by a cover-up when he saw one —
it's not abstracts we die of, but details —
he slipped under logs he used re-building it
and landed in hospital with back injuries.

I asked how you live with constant pain
when *every* day is a back-breaking day.
I was getting emotional. The sky was hot.
I could hear silver eyes rioting in the tree
like a thousand *buts*. They wanted to go.
But if it was about belief, and faith and
the biggest bogey of the lot, justice, God
had that to answer, didn't they think?

I began in jest but something else cut in.
I stood there, querulous and very young.
I saw our mulberries staining their shoes.
So my arms spread wider as if to span
the aching weight of it all: the empty
place between this world and his heaven.
This world is the world I want answered.

But now when I find them at the door
I think of their mulberry-stained shoes
and words which can't explain conundrums
swept in very distant orbits. Now I
say I'm just not interested in God and
justice and bridges. I mean, unable
to bear their eagerness, I lie to them.

Crows: at the Border, Things Increase

                                     On the wall
of the Alterworld, as exemplary life and death
are the strange. And crows. There is no wall
but I have felt it and heard on its other
dead side how we live de-exaggerated
moments, not quite enough cause
and effect, not enough logic not
enough fidgety texture
or feeling.

                         I dream I am sometimes there.
I do not mean I sometimes dream I am there.
Be-sided, where the living are lost without us,
wandering among the silent or the windy lots,
a terror of long faces, and crows sit above us
cawing like cracked sirens, and not flying
in the air. Because it's not signs they
offer, but continuity
and fear.

                               Running on their fast
intelligent feet to peck at carrion the tautological
carrion peck at the pun in this gloomy, this de-
natured life below, is beyond the wall, its exits
aren't physical but divide the two worlds like
a bad prayer. Fear, they caw, and haunting.
Here, look back at the world and listen:
on *this* side of the border the crows
sound like that side.

Heimweh and *Fermweh*

Here
it's raining so hard the puddles are cheap champagne.
There
the low horizon doubles and lifts in sulphurous dawn.
Here
the track you and I walk a millions of years of walking.
There
the city is a spatter of crystals, one becomes a hundred.
Here
a speeding train shuffles its windows like bright cards.
There
its destination, leaving us for it, walking for hurtling.
Here
plunging from light and rain into the vanishing point.
There
the two cross: another train is hurtling towards us.

Creatures of the Alterworld

The Frida-and-Diego Metaphors

Their strange love: the ferret-and-the-frog,
the dove and the lizard, the old goanna then.
Happy to help out, huge and gleaming,
Diegos' penis leaps like a frog.
He shares it with the Communist women
like a good Communist, and with women
generally, like a General.
Frida is hirsute weirdness or the lyric poet
of hair, her ornate dressing and re-assembling
sensuality. Her Trotskyite eyebrows
and hands like revolutionaries.
The art of Frida's plumage flies to canvas
as Diego stares down from his murals
with a girl in each eye: chameleon.
Communists are rarely so much fun.

The Lovers

For all his tall dark handsomes
she knows she can't guess how
reliable his pheromones or looks
will be.
          His testicles are dice.
When she fucks him
two sixes blow her and she comes.
But when she isn't looking
she gets pregnant on two ones.

The Celebrities

When he wakes up on the lounge room floor
she is throwing things. The cats aren't journalists.
There's no money. You're a thicko, she yells in his face.
His penis shrinks so much it is a vacuum, a whoosh!
As the next plate passes closer than she aimed.
She forgets why it started, but then he hits her.
Is it summer or winter? He imagines Homeric
similes, she the fall of Troy, but she gets nostalgic
a day later, she regrets she called the cops.
Money brings back some reality, and cameras.
But come on, they are lyric, not narrative, poets:
they cannot remember anything in any sequence
alcohol has them, and short lines is all they manage,
best the white stuff. Lies, that is. The dark places,
he says, she says, are scary. But *I'm not pressing charges*
moves in them like mime. It's their late-onset
clairvoyance. Yet he is 1.86 and 84 kg to her 55.
Women are tough, he thinks. His penis whooshes.

The Client

Awkward, knowing he should leave
and never have come, he straightens
his jacket and pulls his zip back up
like a launch reversing on its wake.

The Visitant

A horse at the gate come from nowhere.
A horse stands unlike a cow whose weight
bears down on its haunches from each leg
in balance its big gravity low in her long
suspended belly. A horse is leggy has lift
in the muscles and this horse at the gate
has her slim left hind-hoof tilted and light
delicate as a girl her slim limbs and honey
skin and she has no concern at all no self-
consciousness. This tan horse at the gate
no farms near us no public access and yet
she is down at our one gate from the bush
paddocks. With no horses on properties
near us for miles she stands un-saddled
has come from somewhere to stand here
like a question-mark at the gate and wait
for loving attention from me. I am unable
to leave. I am stroking her unable to make
sense of it but moved out of myself as if
this is more real than sensible. The horse
not one bridled and saddled and ridden
to its death by people, no free horse lost,
no bridled horse escaping, so what was
this from my head leaping out into horse,
beside the gate, delicate and all things not
bidden to suffering, or not now. No horse
on the farm for forty years and no visitor
like her before to open me here at the gate
to carry me away from where I am less of
my self than I know now to stand waiting
in love with a horse that maybe isn't here.

Autism and

Wind beat against the house like angry brothers.
A clan undone, past sane, by paybacks, vendettas.
As lorikeets kept on, piercing the buffet-and-roar
rain and swish-wash of cars. I heard a child laugh,
or... ? Out there? Again. I heard and went and saw
a child still in nappies, in rain and wind, grunting
at trees, yelps thin and cold in the obscure. Lifted
up he smelt clean and warm, he smelt of a breast
in this street. He yelped, he uttered, had nothing
of words, betrayals. No family, no story, no sign
of parents, a fireplace, the terrace houses. Niente.
Cars in northern suburbs bullet up onto a house,
rival families: drugs and race relations, none of it.
Dramas and clans, past sane, paybacks, vendettas.
This street wasn't – this child – from somewhere
imprisoned, ransomed. Just careless: a small bird
shaking, or a puppy warm but wild, no words to.
At the third terrace with doorlight I found them,
his own. None of them noticed he had gone. Yet
we stood under their light, alone in all the world,
at the lit end of the corridor. I banged their door
several times, I recall, to bring them: so life comes,
suddenly, quietly amazed, as if to a hallowed child.
To three of them. And me. The keeper of the inn.

Before if Ever a Landfall

The deck of their boat heaves: a column of bleak pilgrims
stands on the back of a mythic animal.
Its different adulterations: if called by prayer or desperation,
if by soundings in their heads,
if by suffering... It comes equally
lifting and sinking. The Beast.

The bridge of a boat is half-theatre half-
control room but no one knows who or what reviews
the under-monster or braces
them against it. All the acts but no rehearsals.
A ship in heavy waves is dragging weight
under their feet. The past drags through them
like love-and-death's sad lines.

A bridge, a wheel, and the long dumb-face
dials and screens. Against abstraction: navigation.
In sunk faith there is the rent-a-skipper
and the hated boat they banked on.
Bad karma is the stink of sewage onboard, the stink
of diesel, sludging water
in the broken hull.
If boats set off and arrive and churn above
their sunken girths...
The animal answering their call is the beast calling to itself.

––––––––––

What is empty? Everything. With no dials, with no
face or figures, no placebos.

The ocean is the opposite of money: it looks
like blinding surfaces of currency, the billions

and billions of billions ...   belonging to nobody.
Nothing but more of itself: that is a definition

of God. Not hubristic howlings, poets or politicians,
full of themselves, unholy men vicious with, but God.

———————

In the morning the sun strides to them over the waves
like models in scattering sequins.

(Who said?): To change worlds, the place you travel *to*
is not a place you will return from. Unless...

It can all be lost. Again.
(Who cares?): That voice, the wrecking ball or the wise one.

Look around you, and the hope dies
like God, but hope returns like travel

from that other place it was
dreaming of. Hope is miraculous. Irrational.

———————

Sunset across the endless waves and hopes
the sun is a red blister.
People who come by boats look like boat-people.
They are disasters' blood, and blisters.

Their eyes are full of ocean but underfoot *is* blood.
The hand you lift to shield your eyes
pink with its inner X-ray
has become the hand of a stranger.

Glass walls dissolve in front of you.
Rain brings a nothingness up close, it taps on
bare heads and darker skins, on you, you, scattering music
on the ocean's address-less ones, rain's
piano of water on the face.
Seven veils lean across the ocean.

The worst politicians in the safest lands but unsafe seats
are beasts, in mortal bodies, immortal machinations:
to win elections… or not risking losing them.
And us, no, not just them, seated, suited. Us.
Don't let them in. Let. Let them, you, us.
Don't. The un-sudden islands, detention, the not-going-away
Ministers of No Heart. Leaking.

Their damned emphatic stresses intruding, trochaic riot:
Arabs, Afghans, Islam, Animal torturing Others.
Black, Brown, Bearded, Bombers, Breeders,
when our moral world blurts out gibberish they open
their mouths and out of their mouths comes the sound of gulls.
Here on the sill and threshold and door
of the ocean. *Just let them.*

Now it opens in front of them. The boat enters.
The loss of centuries or the loss of tomorrows.
This drowning of other-Gods
and the un-wanting-masters. Through the towing door
children wash into darkness.
Then, no longer a door,
the ocean closes.

Driving into Dawn

The world is everything that is the case.
– Wittgenstein

In colloidal light the insects,
dun cars, headlights staring
low and blink-less as snakes.
I began this. So many ages.
When I wake I am driving
and forwards at last, at least,
and shattering sounds aren't
escaping me, or my thoughts
stop lurching like animals.
Steering the last few corners
slowly through a small town
: its dark main street bereft
as an old church flowerless
in Lent.

    Something
whitens my peripheral sight
then is gone. The buildings
have lost pub-brawl awnings,
are head-butted, and leaning.
Several figures stand half in
the gloom, half in blackness.
They are half-cards, the half-
watch, and turn towards me.
Half-man.

  I learnt to drive at
fourteen. I have been driving
fifty years. For the first time
I know what I'm doing. I am
not going to be judged. I had
thought to stop here but now
I keep on. Put a roundabout

behind me. I drive to the east.
With no light except my poor
headlights considering a road
of death: this stony bitumen,
slump-shoulder, leprous skin.
But so, indifferently, up a gear
and gone.

    The flecks of blood
I saw briefly lit by street-lights,
a red of intent too dark to see
again. Uphill, up night, down.
I had never belonged here but
the pain won't stop. A leaving
behind, and a low stammering
from the left rear tries to tell,
something I cannot, will not,
hear.

    Death is different at night.
The sound it made, the lurching.
Lost as I was, can it be I lost all
tense? World of leaving become
world of arriving.

     I am answerless.
But oh my heart I am homesick.
Heimweh, fermweh, I'll find you.
Photons arriving, photoblinding
: pale light I will gently call dawn
enters the tree tops and so enters
me. I am entering the next world.
Cluster-bombs of birds go off in
threes. Bird-song, bird-sight, bird.

Smithy Again Again

He stares at a long fish trap, at a fish like a stent.

He floats to the surface, the kid throwing water
is himself on the bank of the river.
History gone.
The bridge he crashed through, and the car stolen.
He can remember it, and the swoon of currents
at his face, and the daylight
increasing upwards
breaking through the surface like a windscreen.

The road was before and was after and was dry.

Now he has decided he is of all things thirsty.
It isn't far to walk there: a service station cafe,
a petrol company he cannot name.
Later
he realises the people bent over their burgers
were all single.
The road was a mirage.

The road led to a tent village in the distance.

When they ask him his name he tells them
it was a name of beating metal. He can not
think what else. For long months of daylight
he lives with them
but when they mention nights and the months
ahead, the road becomes rain.

The road, pitched over with endless small boats.

Passing among them the stronger ones the colours
of his suburbs, their hulls, the blue, the sails,
the single occupants.
Rippling like rolls of bobbing plastic, electrical wiring
in the rain. Wind and twirling but on his way he sees
no shadows.
People move aside to let him through.

In a long room men in coloured shirts are drinking.

And they stare at him, asking
where have you been mate it's your shout.
They are noticing his water-white skin.
Then they are talking and drinking and
staring past him at nothing
at the nothing that will not be changed.

His ex-wife is gone now, she will not return.

Asking him where have you been it's your shout
they were, they are, somehow his friends again,
now he cannot know them. You're alive mate.
They are suddenly smiling
they lean towards him in recurrences he'd never
noticed in them. Love, or mates, he understands.

Palingenesis. They touch his eyelids.

The Making and Resisting Eye

Both of us looked over the edge. Brief vertigo.
I scanned fifty storeys of black stone and you
saw down a cliff-face of reflective glass.
Nature and nurture. Cross-over. Who knows?
Height can do this to us. And planes
crashing into the sides of mountains, buildings.
Sleep or the right drug does CGI for us
because detail only matters if the eye lets it
blur past, reality not literal, not the screen's
where everything gets made, but wasted
because we see it.
          No gauge or digital device
reads the sublime. At heights my heightened pulse
pumps analogue which only might be awe,
if awe is change.
          Salt wind rushes at my face.
City air unexpectedly cold this high up
chills yours. I see small pills of cars and lights.
You, volcanic fractures and boulders, the waves.
Cross-over. We must be ready for change.
When the eye understands the leg-strain
of climbing, the blue neutering the blood
adrenaline wills down into the muscles
hurting up. How to feel enough. Of what?
A cat leaps onto my desk and leans against my face.
This more than mountains. The self can hold it.
Oxygen is barrel-rolling through me as cliff
or 50th floor. It's way beyond my history,
yours too.
          Looking down I am surrounded
by the *impossible*, dark matter, its 98% of everything,
on my face, on my hands, all around and through me
this immensity of the impossible, against
the mere trace
of our possible world our made and modal
building of what we must.
I must resist it to death.
Or embrace it.

Un Certain Regard

A silent overhead of seamless filming from a helicopter
flowing like clear dark water a river above the city
opening another movie. Never low-rise, Paris, or Rome,
it must glorify and make sublime (add sombre music)
or vertiginous New York, Los Angeles, Shanghai,
Hong Kong – the distant streets, America, regardless.

I run my bare hand
down the rough-stone columns at Circus Maximus.
I raise my right hand, run my palm down
the column. Lift my right hand, fingers spread as if
from panic, down the column and slowly regard
three people walking, but only two of them touching.

I prefer the water colours of Richard Tuttle, pastel
washes over oily Freud, his clotted cream his colour
nudes. Minimalist feels honest by comparison
regardless of people saying: Oh, that's just
kids' stuff, you can't beat a good portrait.
(If only he didn't paint womens' you-knows all the time.)

Centuries of portraits, Renaissance, the tenderness
(that rare, neglected quality) glows, and Dr Gachet's
unforgettable sadness. Painstaking technique
regardless of when, that is given and hidden
mostly in storerooms, unseen, in crypts, in private
chambers where the owners are too old to see them.

I live in face after face, all the centuries of loss.
The stone is real, the camera running silently
as cities slip away underneath. Still.
I love more deeply in movies that move me,
lost to it, regardless, than in moments of loving
while I am living.

Ode Owed to Data

Data you're always naked. What are you doing?
You're raw and you're everywhere
like DNA, but only nerds think you're sexy.
Gigabytes or fugues, I can't order you by weight
though you fill computers. Or you cover walls
like ivy ripped away from the bricks.
You are Kepler the prover of our solar centripitus.
Or you are daggy and professorial.

Some of you makes sense like words beside words
inside the huddle of sentences,
hope and doubt knotted together
trying to mate. Mate! You're a snake pit.
Six-dimensional as a pack of physicists
or like a worm-hole through darkness
or the way a sentence slithers on itself.
Air chills in your fangs and your facts are cold.

In your so-coolness you return from space
intact across distance, tiny as a billion haiku
ideograms and fragments we alone interpret.
Without us data you are nothing.
I feel important. I feel like a drink.
Two different feels, like hope and doubt. Get it?
What probability is that, data? 50%?
Liars and saints mumble in corridors of hope
and doubt, as you lick them, or luck them out.

Rain falls everywhere upon the earth like hunger
its surface shimmering with instinct.
Meteorological data is never weather
its impact like tiny scales, its long street like a snake.
I stare at you for hours on end, your imagery.
Weather charts as gigabytes of wet ontology?
Rain, light, everywhere reducible to you, data
– but know thyself? And beyond knowing?
I look into a windless forest, the sun high,
and see the opened score of your symphony:

sound written on silence
and, oddly, silence written on silence.

Then I count up the beauty, talent and luck
you never gave us. We won't forget. Never-was
and never-had are difficult emotions. Not easy,
data, not in your DSM of tags, your hiding-behind
impersonal graffiti. Un-noticed on the big wall.
Now don't take it personally... See past it.
Chance, or liability, and down to data our parents
left us at birth, not death. The one will
we never wanted and your odd unselfish love
of all of us equally.

Never mind. Someone will be soppy and dishonest
and tell us it doesn't matter, love. Tell us
the insufferable sin of sop: everything happens for a reason.
Data, you are the number not the suffering, of millions.
Suffering is everywhere, in data and not.
We are among the lucky the unlucky never had.
It could be true. Useless unless we know.
Data is a blind date. Yes, you.
You can make a concentrated effort and nothing
come of it. We do. What your books don't say
would fill books.

Personals

1

for Ceri

Overnight the smell of coffee disappears in the cafe
unlike the smell of fish in a fish shop.
Whether or not he smells of alcohol.
Now she opens the front door early,
turns the lights on, puts her palms on the heating pipes
in the kitchen, waiting, then sets up for him.
There is a first time, for this Hillsong alcoholic,
when she opens the front door early
and finds him asleep in the back room
smelling of alcohol. Because he never went home.
He evaporates in the room.
Even then he tries to touch her. She, his waitress,
managing the till, her hands on the money, the key.
Who in her, not his, paralytic clench
writes out the staff roster for those girls left
who will still work, avoiding his hands
if not his words. He is the smell of fish in the cafe.

2

for Jac

Yeah it's funny about Smithy it was his missus
did you hear about her? No? She told me
because we were all booked to go to a bloody concert
tickets over a hundred bucks so jesus nothing
to chuck away in a hurry. His missus wouldn't go she said
it was too much he drank too much she had to leave.
And anyway they are broken up now but
he said he was over her he just got tired of her
she said it was too much that he drank too much
when he wasn't at work. Said it was always with us!
Said he'd gone missing. Been several months.
She was pretty bloody shirty about us leading him astray.

We all drank too much it was our
bloody fault. I said look hon
we never seen him after work ever and he doesn't drink
with us. And we haven't seen him at work for yonks.
Her mouth just opened.
We're all a fucken mystery mate we really are.

3

for Carter

When the man walked past them they never looked up.
Three young women from the dog's home
volunteers
sitting and laughing on the grass under a plane tree.
The small brown dog between them
so happy
he was trying to talk and not leap
never looked up from the women as the man limped past
across to the walking track
to the shops for the cigarettes they told
him he must give up.
He's not a magician and would need at least briefly
three young women from the land of the living
volunteers
to sit and dote on him and laugh in the sun
to replace his comfortable and completely
silent cigarettes.

4

for a former self

After the abattoir is closed
what he says to me is this, that it came to him
the same way one of his mates went down
to Billy Graham and gave up his life for all
that Jesus stuff. I have to half-believe him.
He looks at his hands (his hands) and looks up:
he says he saw the banks rise up from the lake

like the roughened skin around his fingernails.
How much older, older than *he* was, he thought,
these hands of his, more life and death on them
than is passing, or falling, in his thoughts
and slower feelings.
Said he saw something moving
hundreds of metres away, something emerging
from an African documentary: graceful animals,
dozens of them, moving in file on the furthest bank
of Lake Somethingorother, walking from right to left.
Calm, unhurried beasts... except they were cattle,
and sheep, and pigs, ordinary farm animals filing past.
Thousands now, tens of thousands, more, more than
any thousands of them. He had stared at animals
for 25 years. For 25 years he hadn't seen them.
He looks out into the distance.
I ask him what he did, what happened, and he says
Mate, you wouldn't believe it...
He looks, he looks at me for a long time, then says
What do you reckon?

5

for Haydn

Chess Master. Stunned after heart attack
you are much less the king than the old horse
propped up against the bank of pillows,
the tubes attached to you remind you of the future
you may no longer want
to run.
Your career ends like this,
the Chinese family surrounding your hospital bed:
their boy genius has given you, his teacher,
his chess-winner's trophy,
held up under your left arm like the child
you never had.
It is something at least
that you smile, too tired, too knowing, briefly regal.

6

for Tim

The day is pinched in like hay into a baler
and compressed, released, the mechanism slow
and crushing, repeating, the hours of a week
are dropped in the paddock to dry. It could mean
mild heat, blue, anecdotal skies above the trees ...
stubble fading as the sun drops into smoke.

But on the gravel road above the hay paddock,
driving more slowly past the man baling
so he can sticky-beak, the neighbour sees how much
he cut this year. And if rain comes, comparing
his own, which is hardly begun.
                                        But the tractor
is stopped, the man must be clearing a jam, the baler,
he notices, still turning. He sees the man's arm
lifted up, straight, but his head seemingly inside
the chute, the flywheel turning, very slowly
crushing.
            The neighbour vaults the fence
and races over.

Into Excavation: the Women's Hospital

The hospital excavation: a drug-sided drop.
No babies yet broken waters lie in the clay.
You try outstaring: the hectare, thirty metre
depth into the earth: in front of you, below.
Absence. People stop to stare into its hinge.
Then blink, as they leave, unable to sustain
the eye to absence. An excavation outstares
us. Deep Ist does this. What is, isn't. Dost
drills foundations and every week concrete
grows one floor of sanity, busy to ordinary.

No, listen, I mean it. This is a space-station
engineers and construction workers lean in,
vacuum collapsing the body *inside* the mind.
Their storeys chasm but are not yet storeys
deeper, or above, in ghosts of the blueprint.
Dost grows into itself on images of Ist and
so incarnates the object, then it is enduring.
Its soul has gone, as yours, too, in watching.

Down inside the basement, being Ist returns
by emptiness, as greyness of concrete levels
Dost keeps lifting into a women's hospital:
until people walk behind flowers, the faces
drawn too close for birth or death to recall
of the other world, the alter. Etherised. Or
where they have parked the now irrelevant
car, on a floor, or floors, below you, above,
there it is. Finished. Object. The thing itself.

On the Level

In my Father's house are many mansions

The *Ground Floor* built through everybody's life
has above it Four Levels.
Level 1 is where I went.

You remember your own
associations of childhood, your home,
that summer afternoon the sun whirring along the corridor
as Procul Harum played
A Whiter Shade of Pale
others have remembered, it was a memory song.
Your father burnt your favourite toy
and stood unsmiling in your room.

This anti-nostalgia like anti-pastoral! The only sense is smell.
The air is foul or flowery, cooked, caramelised … then burnt,
a smokeless smoke.
Roses overpower you, the yeast of her throat,
you think you remember her!
the garden enters you but no garden.
Freshly baked bread, bacon cooking but no splutter
of oil in the pan, no eggs, now a roast duck,
an open drain.
Disconnected from their source, from each
these smells are the room in the room
on *Level 1.*

Next door, taste: of kitchens, that varnished duck,
the bacon, drool, as these lie on the chemical
the wet and dry senses live on your palate
as separate as notes in music you might eat
but never digest. It is the mad sense
alone, lost from sense.
Pig intestines slip on your taste buds, Swedish rotten fish
and durian and whale blubber, flavours
you'd never want to meet
rise in you, this room. Taste rushes you, more than you
with its everything that lived.

Footsteps stamp along the floorboards above you,
the sounds of kissing, sweet-talking, conversations,
leaves rustling as a front approaches, then rain on the roof.
Cawing of crows, the bird-call not the bird
the tick not the clock
the sound of a joke and it's a long joke you might laugh
at, but the joke itself,
which is human, stays on *Ground Floor* with the humans.

Jack-hammers shatter like death-rattle-angulating, voice-over
dubbing, the blind make sense of it
hear car alarms as verb, the deaf — nothing in their sweet spot.
A boxing match thud and grunt the hiss of sweat.
The wailing of mothers but not
their dead sons back from a war, their daughters
suffering in childbirth, crying, but absent
as pathos, like possessions on this level
stay with the living.
Without context, none of this means anything.
Like babies crying
except babies crying is all body and isn't here.

In the next room deafness is a country for the seeing:
you see his mouth enunciating silence
perfectly
the syllables of a poem. Beckett's *Not I.*
Truck lights through a country town at night
flash in the shop windows
window   window   window
truck   truck   truck.
A car smashes through the railing and plunges
into a river. Coloured wiring.
Bird egg blue, the blown end of a Lee-Enfield,
no war but a windmill turning and pumping nothing
like Duchamp's nude descending a staircase
without moving.

Doubt envelopes you like a parachute
sinking into you, then opening: your new house,
a truck full of furniture arrives and opens
and you stare into it, stupidly.

Empty of all emotion, you and reason, you (and   ?)
stranded between local and international.
A woman, flat-chested, her lips porcelain, you glow
as she embraces you
she sees bubbles in cloud chambers but you can see
the brilliant villa upon the hill
where the world ends.

Fish gasp on the water's edge, their gills
are small accordions, a man held together with black thread
sewn through his arms and cheeks.
His face is dark, hair like a doormat,
one small cup of Chinese tea held to his lips.
A single wall of bricks painted blue
and dead airmen in the trees. Pathologist in a white gown,
creatures standing under trees.

Kicked and punched, you are stroked and kissed,
you have an orgasm in the dark
where only touch exists, as strange a thing as this?
Your body is opened up and operated on but knowing
you feel nothing but anaesthetic's
nothingness. It is very expensive.

Out from the cloud chamber and Hadron collider
the Higgs boson is waiting, the dark matter the impossible
rushing through concurrent images and senses
the elements
become heavy,
and possible,
and are body, and time enters them
with before and after and with Ist.
The world of *Level 1*
returns to us
the *Ground Floor*, the Alterworld we live in.

On *Level 2* there is nothing but reflections.
Namaste
the lift doors opening take you up, close, then open.
Reflections live without the mirrors and windows.
All the images are flat, most are side-on

cubist and confused, Horus all-seeing but here
numb as old Pharaohs their servants
faces and feet flat to the side.
Standing blank-faced, the striding, the cars, the trees, a cat
walking like a fish.
Backgrounds but no locations.
The laws went through a mangle and came out flat.

Mirrors show us to ourselves and to you who used them.
A woman crying, her face resembles plants,
a man bawls like a heart full of blood.
Bathroom selfies, breasts and bums full frontal and
side-on: belly out and belly in!
2D as playing cards or CT scans.
Men with erections, women leaning into their faces
applying make-up. A nerve twitches under the skin. Snap.

Reflection here is repetition. Narcissism.
Wanting taller, wanting pretty, wanting beautiful, this
desire in the flat and futile.
You look at yourself in the mirror of the mirror
and recursion multiplies you like flat flies.
Perspective is like insecticide
the fat image looked at by the thin.
Namaste.

Level 3 is empty. It is not even relative. Empty.

Level 4 is music.
Level 4 is the counterpoint in red.
Bach or punk, Ska or scat, the same here, you hear
separately again as the senses in the rooms.
The sinking ship, a plunging Airbus, cars crashing.
None of that.
This is where music comes from and returns.
Its elsewhere is here.
Its sad diaspora its celebration of the highest orders
we comprehend. Not know. As close to Absolute,
nothing higher, its upper level consciousness
exceeds consciousness.
In everyone. Grace, essential on the human floor,
is travelling. It travels here.

Three Never-dreams

The Last Key of Marienbad

My grandmother stood arm in arm with old Egypt.
The sand, stone, her favourite polka-dot clothing.
Her manner, knowing, was the doubtless manner
    of one who is right like a pharaoh's leopard
    is right.
A dreamer is a reader of the insides of dreams.
There's something dreaming-Egypt outlives us
like bad interior design, and sarcophagi, but she
    was very still:
an authority that is a quiet half-love/
half-aloneness, of the one who is never alone.

She brought a weird scenery: a temple, a bas-relief
of side-on faces leaning pike-nosed to right or left.
But the pink granite of the temple looked more
like a multinational insurance building,
                      its side-on faces
more of a board directors' meeting after the GFC.
Until she lifted that irksome thing of dreams, a key.

Of course I told myself she held up the possibility
of wisdom. And perhaps she did: the key, the wall,
codes and nudges.
        She was dead by then and dead-
expert as a muse who couldn't have said any of it
when alive.
       It was happiness and hope done quiet,
not the sort of thing a poet gets amazed at: don't
write a poem about it,
she advised, only Seamus
could, perhaps, do it justice. Heaney, and a key?
It was an old-fashioned dream, after all, and she
was a hundred and three.
        When slotted in the wall
it turned my poor amnesia. But this was twenty
years ago and I break my word only now, and let

her 'wise old woman' turn to me. Turn in me.

I was the temple and the key. I didn't like that.
If I tired of fighting against life – I was to turn it…
The day was sunny, glary even, against the granite.

There were no phoney long bodies in short skirts,
the men and women, no whacky lace-up sandals but
I was frozen into that stillness like the garden scenes
of *Last Year at Marienbad.*
                          No longer Egypt
it was a black and white film.
It was lit by reflector boards.
It was almost ah-and-gothic
music, repetitious phrases and reversals,
and the arch
hesitations like (but not) an effing TV cheffing series.
Buckets of fake chords, grimaces over undercooked
unconscious … But its walls made patterns like silent
instruments, and after so much silence,
it felt like the muse of geometrics.
The key fell from the wall like a battery from a torch.

She spoke and I knew what her words meant but
nothing of her words came through the light into
the morning.
                Revelation is never a line of words if
out of context. Had she been embalmed too hard?
Had they hooked her brains out through a nostril
and left her wandering half-stoned in the desert
mythologies? Older than her Old Testament.
More opaque even than that film of Marienbad.

The sun rose like a blob in a lava lamp. I waited
for it to fall. Side-face is po-face, after all. I saw
a bandaid on her wrist, and her goitre as it had:
grown into a melon on her throat.
The closest thing she had to God.
After hope, the sub-text.

Journey Back to the Father

Sometimes I help him balance along the endless platform.
I note he has wet trouser cuffs and his right knee is damp.
He keeps walking into the CBD from inner suburbs along
a platform which repeats its stairs its signs its bench seats
but never reaches the city and never meets the schedules
and trains screech and scream and lay our ears back, as if
scouring the air like Raptor 44s, but stopping hours ahead
somewhere. He stumbles, my father (and I catch him), old
now but not as old as when he died, and in greater health,
it must be said:
– God, it's hot. Is it still summer? Christ, I'd love a cold beer.
– OK. Let's find a pub or a bar along the platform and stop.
– Nah, they only sell coffee. It's like bloody Melbourne.
– You don't like coffee?
– When did I ever like coffee? I want a beer but every time
I walk to the train, it's like this, it's just coffee shops. This
is what happens here. It happens all the time.
We stumble past its fluoro-lit, and brown-fronted shops all
selling coffee, not cafes, just awnings sagging over counters.
This my first time helping him, his damp and baggy trousers,
his black shoes scuffed from the daily platform, a slow-walk
marathon, the endlessness of it. And trains that never stop.

Coffee   Coffee   Coffee   Newspapers   Coffee

We arrive on a platform opening out into sunlight the rails
stained from piss, and unhappy passengers on the benches
under the sign: NO TRAINS TODAY! NO SERVICES RUNNING !
My father is not a swearing man but right now he growls
like graffiti, front-bar ugly, but no beer, no train, nothing.
Nothing. Then we start walking back, shoes, stumbling,
the brown coffee shops and their brown shutters down.
Stumbling, shuffling, leaning forward, all the way back.
He never said it but somehow he wanted God. Instead:

Closed   Closed   Closed   Closed   Closed

The Present

I enter the world again and all its words
turn towards me with their faces
blotched. They mean what they mean.
And what they might and what they don't.
Should I even try to understand?
Me, I am the foolish. Of We.
Of asking the questions.
Of Now.

Ist and the Poet

These are my tricks.

And if I am inside its placement this is the perfect photograph of stillness,
its composition classical. Its colours sit and light is set to body temperature.

Shadows in a room are leaking away from the five strong surfaces of light:
arms of chairs in arcs are horizontal water-light lake-ing the table-top.

It looks like a room I have forgotten. Unless I am noting its brightness
of possibles, my muse is sleeping – my face of Brancusi marble.

But look – the blood pressure monitor is silvered and Cartesian.
It waits. My blood is invisible, impossibly quiet. Ist.

The upper surfaces of forgotten apples are wrinkled and white
doughnuts of apple-light. My glasses on the table are blind.

But each lens is the same: a window and a street lamp hang
upside down, they bulge in the black frames like art.

...

No no enough of this. The phone is ringing
here in my head. Answer Answer. It says
something else is happening, not this
layered light and language stuff. Disfluent.
  This and this and the pataphor.
  Un-able to resist being solipsist.
  Something is arriving. Rips at the fake
texture we are, language is, the surfaces ...
and rips at, tries to return from where it is not.

...

The blood pressure monitor is dumb and quiet.
But later I will attach it to my bicep and pump.

The heat in this room is like a body carrying its 'do not touch'
kind of instrument. I feel it against me, tempting, like a cat.

The trees are black as rags torn along their rougher edges
dense against orange bleeding from the horizon.

You walk into the room and speak, but only the words you
use are said. Not these behind, after- and before-words

of mine. The silence, my brain, the chemistry I see with,
pre-exist me. I am un-first-personed.

But. This is the altering.

His Alterworld as Counterpoint

for Glenn Gould

He places his medications on the table.
Quick quick quick.
The air re-arranges around them. They are notes and names,
they are anxiety and thrill, they are dangerous
adolescents. The gang of them. He stays home
to be with them.

Gould as Gould. Notorious for bent-over playing Bach
at astonishing speed and every note in the gang
in stilled position. The sadness of his clarity
the singing rain the provocations
of fast notes Dost Dost Dost

At night after gunning through Bach again again again
finding voices no one else can play apart
he pushes Bach aside   Black and lacquered his beloved
                                          CD 318 Steinway its lid open
to study his beautiful pharmacy. No, not everyone can strike
a Bach rote and as limpid in the air as Ist
but anyone can swallow the internet's
million illnesses. Amazingly,
each in your own likeness...   The Pharmaceutical (...) Almanac.
                                   The what? Real Wish to cure Want.

From the outside, if to any of us this looks like guilt
each tablet taken is accepting of innocence:
yours and the tablets – they have the kindness
of pets.
        Maybe your house is over-run with them,
as you are over-run with them, their legato
their long effortless running and sleeping
passacaglia of tablet-cats.
Their key of bliss.   Hypo chon dria: a sexuality of syllables
                                   their lists and Ist

Waltz 1: the famous Glenn Gould is conducting
with his left hand raised instead of the right.
The world he holds aloft invisible Other of music
there, invisible in his fingers, the music of music.
The orchestra has to ambi-dexterise to keep
in time. Outside him, out-conducting him.

Everything he did was by script and score.
Arms plunging through interviews he wrote
both parts of: subject and counter-subject
he dared, was dauntless, even for Menuhin
saying : "But Yehudi, I know what you think"
when Menuhin departed from The Script.

The hypochondriac spams himself again and again.
He has firewalls in his computer but none in his brain.
There are packets of coloured pixels denying it.
Suspicious symptoms the inky unintelligible score.
Only the endless systolic talking talked.
                              Schumann? Schumann was a sissy

If an unworldly you stood outside the you as cold
as the mirror-body: as flat, outstaring you
unimpressed by chemistry or sentiment
who knows what it ever thought about music.
If it thought about illness, and if it thought
in the fugue of curing you.
                              There is a Ghost called Glenn Gould

Waltz 2: The jovial snake-arms of a Glenn Gould
rear head high and strike into the keys.
They lift the light of his face they hit coolly as the glass
outstaring.
                    Any impurity is bled off
in endless noises: yet another Gould is the awful
humming, Bach is the playing, the Gould in greatcoat
and scarves, shunning a live audience.
                              Live performance is a blood sport
Never an audience — just someone to *listen*.

After scalding his long hands for half an hour
in the studio musician's bathroom basin
the doctor steps out hands raised in the air
in a studio set up for filming   Its walls white as aspirin
for and from Bach's pregnant presence
and with his pink and scalded hands
he delivers the many voices.

Autumn. A woman three floors down
who wipes each surface clean, twice,
counts to ten, wipes the surfaces
again, wears the same as always
overcoat and as she locks unlocks
seven times the front door to leave
notices a bruise on her left hand.
Notices next to the letterboxes
32 leaves, yellow as medication.
This and this. Must go back inside
again, treat the bruise, then wipe,
count, and check the medication,
lock, leave. Same as or alteration?
The devil is in the detail, ah, but
which? No sign of genius, in this.
No Gould is. It might have been.

Waltz 3: The beguiling arms of Glenn Gould
rise and fall as his left lifts and swirls
up and down her silken body his greatest
love: music the ghost he waltzes with
like the undead, music not a currency
but blood, and he feeds on it, arms raised.
To be nothing but the empty medium
from composer to listener,   A man in black on a broken stool

nothing in the way ...
of Beethoven from

here   to   here

of Bach from

here   to   here

of Gould from

here

Nembutal	Phenylbutazone	Sepicil
Gantarin	Thorazine	endless
Trifluroperezine	Luminol	somethingomycins
Pentobarbital	Inderol	Librase
Aldomet	Fiorinol	Butalbital
Bonadine	Naproxen	Valium
Hydrochlorothiazide	Septra	Aspirin
Indocin	Allopurinol	

to *here*

By size and a near phobia of the colour red
the Scholar and his pretty Placebos
eggs at breakfast and nuts and pills.
This radio producer, this fuguist of voices.
Talk and talk and talk and blood pressure
forces of and he dotting as contrapuntal
polyphonic at home in the snow at pace
pissing, always, its music. His dog, his cat.
The cat baroque, the dog romantic.

When the police came the father
had stared at his son like murder:
One word from you, and you're d…
The cops scratched around then
noted her discoloured face like a
question, she answering nothing
except in grunts just one key up
past silence. They sighed, hitched
their gun belts. That boy clearly
crazy. And pulling at his clothes

in pinches like they hurt his skin,
and grimacing, eyes fast as fleas.
This boy who had it memorised:
every curse every physical taunt
and punch and now the number
of rivets on the cops' belts could
tell it back note or rivet perfect -
but won't. To think Bach wrote
The Well Tempered Clavier
for *his* children to practise form.
Never this. Suppose it had been.

The "Martian" Gould. Alone-ness is the longest Ist.
It is savant and only streams from him like
performance in a sealed studio. The few
he phoned for three hours from 3am on.
Now his head was heavy, his playing *felt*.
Just listen. He lived as Glenn Gould inside
Glenn Gould and Bach's perfection
and with all the things
that were not wrong with him.
Until all the things that were not wrong with him
all the medications that he took for them
seeped over his lips like red rain
a stroke and a stroke and a stroke.

[Now on YouTube they rave
and criticise him. When he plays the Goldberg
what you hear is Dost
what you feel is Ist.
His Prelude and Fugue #1 in C major
is travelling at 61,400 kmh
(he nods approval) through
stellar space in
Voyagers 1 and 2.
Un-altered music
un-changing space]

Shots

Waiting room

Next! Murmuring. Another life is torn
off the pad and given to you. Perhaps.
How many years you laugh and suffer.
Fate is *too slow*. But you take it, thanks,
with love even. It is your nature after
all, to live fast and ignore the risk, the
delirium of your tremens! But look:
the sky is the comedian of colours
the roof-stalls are full
of laughter.

Point of view

When I had my vasectomy
my second wife
said she wanted to watch.
Some people
have thought this odd.
I disagree.
But it might have been
if my first wife
had.

The endless healing of

Recognition, look upon your race.
No causation, increasing, intransitive.
The temperature peaks at 44
and day splits open, its
heatedness flies everywhere
from air to head the people
outdoors, parted from themselves the butter
-pupae they see at newstime, indoors,
of cooling crimes and reasons.
Recognition, this is all yours,
you are the country of
all of us, the language.

The air takes no breathers today
it is only heat, only surrender.
You know us hatching, incarnate,
your knowing is the shadow on us,
incomprehensible but
the power beyond us, bonding us.
Short of answers, cracking open
half-blind in the sun.
Recognition, say something,
how we began isn't necessary,
but of our ending.

Death speaks your language

Not true if Death is deaf
Death is all of and no language
no speech at the end of us

Death has ropes from each world
over its shoulders
drags some of us and wrestles others
Samson-backed.
We perform un-speakable things
Death does to us

Oh this is nonsense
Death isn't anything or like anything
Because of logic what Death is
Death isn't

Coastal

The boat coming in on the swell
is limping like a professional:
great regularity. I'm impressed.
It keeps this up even when it's moored.
A man revs up a dinghy to come ashore.
Its thin, nasal, uninteresting sound
makes the wind bored, makes the wind
shift and stir behind the houses.
I could go on and on like this.

The Parcels Arriving

The parcels keep arriving in twos or threes
like cartons of heady shiraz from a wine club
for the connoisseur, or the drunk. But no clink, no weight.
These parcels arriving.
I must be some kind of tractor beam attracting them
towards me. My mouth opens in a square.
The parcels sit there
unlovely and dumb.
I slit open the heaviest among them but all I find
is dust, a box filled with flying space for moths.
Another parcels holds reams of paper with a letterhead
of the letter S.
The third box opens onto a dying tracery and nerve
like un-learning a first language it has left there
in spider web.
Now I don't
even try: they are as strange as guests at a wedding,
standing in groups, not yet drunk.
Like symptoms of secret raptures that I lost and
forgot. Are they mimetic fallout
sent from past actions still lying in Limbo?
Now they sound like
peacocks in a courtyard.
There are several white boxes stacked up like a hospital
building, with fluoros, and white walls
and help! help! inside them.
I must consider this: parcels that arrive may not be gifts.
I hear in one the slow rustle of shoulder-wings.
Have I ordered angels? I may be vain and even foolish
but surely I would
remember that.
I take them to the back yard and begin burning them.
I crush them, I bend them over whatever it is
hunched inside them
and the smoke bursts up black and white and vermillion
into the foliage then up over the tree-line.
It doesn't smell like cardboard burning.

So I open one.
There are love letters, mine to her, and there amazingly
hers in reply, letters I have never seen.
Another: diaries addressed to me from my silent father,
all he felt and had wanted to say but couldn't
when he was alive.
A late *True North*.
A box of birth certificates, two that claim me.
A box of hurt, its voices going on and on.
In this past I feel my future shifting.
There are no more boxes.
At the window I am watching for the next delivery,
my heart pounding. For one day, then another.
But now that I know
they stop arriving.

By the Time They Found Adele

for Adele Bailey

In her well or mine, in her transsexual sex
detection diary, and Sgt Dennis Tanner's
words lay in the black ink beside her.

Tiresias/Adele, who broke down to her bones.
Her man's bones, and her silicone, her numb
sloughing body nakedly unavoidably the story.

But on a farm nearby, poor Jennifer Tanner.
Yes, the cleverest ever of suiciders, who
shot herself right through the palms of both

hands, and who so amazingly outside herself
shot herself twice in the head with a single-shot
bolt-action rifle. Is she in the Guinness Book

of the Dead? *Yes, yes*, the policemen said.
So much goodness and truth and then …
Tiresias is blind enough to see. The box and dice.

And Adele's silky implants that ID'd her.
Adele who spoke The Well Mouth of her poems
artesian seeping to the endless prose of oceans.

*yeah I was belly-up before Underbelly. to be ID'd by what I was not. it takes
imagination. my implants were the saddest eggs. but listen. like Tiresias small
birds rise in my throat. this is what I see. everyone rises through the surface
of the earth.*

A Night-long Performance of Peter Brook's *Mahabharata*

Ceaseless going over and going over swayed
her voice into millennia, the millennia in her throat
swayed in me, its sad and ceaseless zaftig of tone
rose and fell under the violins chugging, in unison.

Yes, chugging, not romantic. The Pandava brothers.
Lament here, the drum-spats, the harmonium's
square book of the Vedas opening and closing.
Earth. Death. When I woke from it millennia
had come, and left. Timelessness is greater time.

At dawn in the local quarry we usually ignored
the cliffs were cut open by Vedic wars:
gelignite has nothing on this. Opened I was/we were.
Peter Brook was a thousand years old in this new
Sanskrit English International Cast
iron Epic.

His Arjuna seized us, he was handsome *and* epic
and everyone fought beside him, side against side,
but no victory a victory: we were dying to know
of epic knowing and to mourn for what is real
in what is not. Nine hours and centuries
is a lot of dying of the not really real.

But at six am the sun stood up amongst us
and threw the rug from its shoulders.
Mahabharata. Just the sound of it is glorious.
We had done right and been wrong, been honourable
and weak, loyal and venal, heard the tragedy of the wise

and the foolish, and felt big quarry tears, the terrible,
compassionate arrows of a real Mahabharata
plunge through us.
So filled and fooled, now we were filing home
into the world.

Bush Walk

Carrying food in our backpacks
like organised people walking into the bush.
Into the sand-filled acres and bush-land
across the river from the farm, where my world is
just a hardly-fenced paddock like a vast spare room
gaping unroofed under sunlight, full of trees and junk:
a broken-down car circa 1950, once Al Capone, once
50s television, not even once driven here
but towed from a clearing sale to this, and dumped.
Its chromium headlights
dulled out, the body the colour of rocks and dust
and exploded leather seats upright on the sand beside it.
A tractor, three ruined ploughs, discs bent into coffee-rock.

In cities no carcases to consider.
To a point. Not the final, not the actual.
A dry-docked yacht a skeleton of a cow its perforated hide
curved as a bench from years of sitting
wasted and worn smooth, but not a living cow
left now. Nothing to scare or provoke.
The farm was on irrigation paddocks and dark soil.
Bush air is living silence. Meteors may have shovelled
this sand, eons been and gone, left nothing obvious
not even minerals. This sand is empty, nothing
except ants in it. Peppermint trees, a few jarrahs
their old and miserable causes of continual thirst.

Now. Here. Upslope at the log, we sit after checking first
in the shadows, and listening, for the snakes
I never mentioned to you.
In New York they call it the taxi-cab position: you
ease down onto me, astraddle. There is something
indefinable about coming in open bushland.
Our skin is barer, more nakedly erotic, the voyeur
skies down over us, the juices seem infinitely cooler
but run more freely.
Of course I planned this rural moment.
In a world of accident we might as well load it our way
as lose it. Who's a monk to simply let it?

The mind is everywhere, un-tagged by name or century.
This place seems nowhere, impossibly us.
Generations who may have stood in this day or place
luminesce inwardly the possible consciousness.
You mention the tea trees waving and
kangaroo paws velvet and brilliant on their stalks
like slim adolescents. Like you slimly on my lap,
your long bare arms over my shoulders.
I live in imagined worlds but I would bring you
with me. I might be dead, or endless, or limboed
where you were not. Instead I bring you to
this temporary world of sunlight and skin,
the sky uppermost beyond us.

More Creatures of Alter

The Flying Thing

Overhead, stuttering
and revving, a Tiger Moth is a 1920s
daydream petalling through air,
child of splutter with an adult of sun,
two-winged, poster-yellow fuselage,
the insides of a steel junk-shop
impossibly aloft, with its coughing
adult pilot and ecstatic engine
of his autistic son.

The Grown-up

When you are your parents
finally, the orphan you left
behind will want to know
who loves an orphan?

The Aged

You feel it when you look at them:
there's a void in portraits of the aged,
the features fall in like an old well.

Before they go all samey,
like babies, the old go honest,
even at their own expense.

Perhaps the tameness of happy homes
infuriates them. Perhaps the wilderness
of illness makes their faces bony

and particular as feet. Vertebrae
adding up their number make mistakes,
it's always less. Names fall off.

As if our brains are put in sideways:
as if the night sky itches with stars: as if
we're wire hangers on a cold rail.

Their eyes know: they will touch
and tell everything: they are driven to touch:
their separateness is too full:

they touch: they are speechless.

Tiresias The Well Mouth

Tiresias striking two copulating snakes
is transformed by Hera into a woman.
A woman who can hear birds singing.
A prostitute. A seer. In seven years she
gets among snakes again, is returned a man.

Zeus and Hera ask this man who was a woman:
who gets the most pleasure in sex? The woman.
Zeus gives him prophecy, Hera strikes him blind.
And still, poor old Tiresias never saw it coming.

At the Disused Drive-in Theatre

At midnight. Its mesh gates sagging and the chain
wrapped in loops which hang like a snake on the frame.
The padlock broken.

(Scene 1)   At the running links of a chain
pulling loose and falling. Crows barking like dogs and real dogs
arching their throats like alligators in the swamp.
Trees that held patches of sunset in their branches
black now, in wind that is pain.

But the sun is silent.
There is no moon.

                          At the other side of what I know. I get inside.
                    The flat screen is stained, broken in dirty pixels
            the sensuous ripple-soles of bitumen lapping forwards in salvos of
                shadow or shockwaves of light-shot, from the projectionist's
                    sullen bunker. Dead grass. Darkness. An iron gate.
                              The smash of windows.

        Metal loudspeakers hang on stands like Darth Vader foreheads
                              louvred with worry, tart-lipped
                    as death. I trip and fall, my jeans tear open at the knee.
            A child. I am that child, bleeding beside his fallen bike.
                I stand and run from the figure behind me.
                      It must be a man. I turn to see…
        I walk into overwhelming waves like a film into a suicide.
                    I see this like insomnia, like my life,
            like any life kept awake when all it wanted was
            to sleep. In wakefulness is worry and insanity.
                    So full of want, as much as murderers want,
        to be. He cried, not for her, they said he said, but for himself.
                (Oh, cry cry cry… the victim! ce'st moi!)

At the booth a door opens. The monster projectors
lean into the vent like mash time at the trough.
From the darkness steps Mr Benchley, the old mute projectionist.
He snaps the main switch:
the projector flares and flashes with fire and light,

he clips on a reel he Brailles the film though its feeds,
a celluloid river gushes – its parallel holes flacker at the gate.
Light eats the images the monster digestion
rattles and rattles.

(Scene 2)

               I am in a darkened hall beside the din of a projector.
           With a hundred students as Lawrence Olivier's *Hamlet*
          flaps and frowns, hugely as neuroses' black and white
indecisions, his face sharp, a steely Prince cut from the lathe of his
       enunciation. Aimed at everything, at all the time inside him,
    the white the world the mind the screen, film as a kind of Dead,
             breeding the living from moments of light.

                    I am there. I am hardly listening
                but I see the hall, the hunched students.
      Olivier the man who could, directing the actor Olivier
             acting as Hamlet, the man who could not.
    If I am real I am the memory of a film, of a play, in a play,
            directed by the actor who acted as Hamlet
who acted as a man
who must murder.

(The Scene)

          In a flashing booth a rhythm calms the horror
        of Hell and murder thrown into light. The three-headed
animal of Adrian Ernest Bailey (the lion the leopard the she-wolf)
            having been irrevocably introduced
             into the world of existing things
            his face so ordinary it blinds us
        held upside down, hands chained behind his back
for 'when she didn't do it right' for rape, for strangulation, for 'who
                has the power now?'
     is offered the lesson of gravity: pure as it is, drowning ...
And mercy: raised vomiting into the breath he broke. Endlessly ...
         In prisons of brick and fear but not one door.

Mr Benchley is staring into his hands. He might be counting...
Then coughs, softly, like a cat.

            The Treacherous, the Malicious, killers
     and extortionists, the bent police, the QCs who could and did,

inserted flat as cards squashed face to face in a garish room
of Piranesi shadow and suggestion, Bill Henson. No compassion,
the chilling concertina crushing in.
Dead-eye politicians who punished and divided refugees and children,
are like hypocrisy dividing, split
in half to stare one-eyed, horrified upon their other half.

The races are held side-by-side and separate
like film passing start-stop through the gate of white:
Geneva Movement, not the Convention,
persisting like pain across the nano-reach, of darknesses
we cannot see in order to see.
The damned, your voices
are Darth Vader from tinny speakers hanging on their stands
your voices are shovel-on-concrete scrape.
Holes driven through walls.

The past is leaning into the clothes of the present.
The past doesn't like mornings. Imagination a blackening sky.
Pain you named us, we put your mask on.
You know there are too many dead to imagine punishment.
Here say its strangle-nouns its gaudy verbs. Its kitsch.
Life's alive, but Hell repeats. Inferno is not a narrative
but a tense: all three at once.

The booth explodes. Night is a shelf of sparks.
The old Projectionist Benchley falls against the door of flames,
and there men's hands pluck him, burning ...

(Scene leaving)
We are so awake we are blind. Of the I obsessed with itself
even sorrow would be truer. To die, to wake.
Weary, I lean back like someone trying to read a bill.
The booth is desolate and dark, the big screen broken.
A chain loose on the ground beneath a sagging gate.
A broken lock.

And suffering? – How we
fall for it.

I look up.
I feel stars on my face.

241

The Drone

Never clear from the job description, the sweaty interview
how through the digital and yogic
he manoeuvres the drone above figures on the ground
his chakra's over-time, his own laws
merely of life and death.
                    Seated out of death's time and place
he levitates thousands of kilometres away
and one above, fire in the heavens, his purpose.
His singular weather and scripture
is data: weighed, calculated, and then released.
Another page of Bible, the Book
of Retribution
is digitised, and checked and then filed.
His coffee under the fluoros in the empty cafeteria
is white: smoking is banned here, banned in the courtyard.
He must wait until he is home,
after the next shift, up, across, the sun, the sand,
thinking of a cigarette.

A Man and a Dog in Morning Fog

Forget those cliches about the sea and sky.
Days are worn out by stupid comparisons.

The dog wants a corner pungent, identified
by layers of dog piss – this one, this one, this.

A hundred metres back a neat black frame
joins a world into place. Is perfectly placed.

No one is there to say this. No one needs to.
A morning can be perfect without comment.

The building might be Italy but it isn't. Day
dampens their shoulders, wet air, or grey.

The man leans into his next step, his mind
elsewhere, or perhaps there, there and not

dragged away by dreams or metaphors, just
weight on the left foot moving to the right.

After a Rehearsal of Handel's *Messiah*

When blinding headlights gave me the wheel:
a car was growing at light-speed behind me
and passing so I saw the big pale curve of it
like a sea creature lit by a bathysphere and soon
disappearing. Then it grew back so fast I was dazed
forced to pass it at speed. It was on ... My interior
flooded with its lunging up, its double spotlights, my head
and shoulders flooded with backlight and this
seen but not seeing that makes you suddenly weak
surging past me, then hard onto the brakes.

Full of young blokes drinking and shouting.
I swung out from their back-end and they cut insanely
across me into darkness, at corners into oncoming cars,
between fear and film I indicated right and still in front
they swung into the off-street as I floored it straight on.
It was worth a try ... even as I saw their black Valiant
emerge from the dust of a spin and full of big six
grunt onto my rear bumper then swing alongside
and ram back like a sling shot into the side of me
missing as I hit the gravel and slid, back, off

the tyre-chop and what was this tearing
music, thinking back on it, onto bitumen that was so
slow now they crash-stalled me to scorching standstill.
Stepping out, one of them seemed to conduct, with his left hand,
the tyresmoke. Like cowboys but fast
they strode two at the front and one at my window.
The smoke was blue gas. They were pale. You can't
guess what they'll want, what burns them enough
for all of this. To discuss the paradigm of road rage?

Heard it all before: shot through the window by a stranger.
But I stayed fast, seeing it: inside a kind of grace.
With Handel hidden in my neck, or was that him
drumming in my chest. Why then, miraculously,
telling me this cowboy's name. Pat Lang.

Two years older in a country school twenty years earlier:
two syllables like his QI spotlights still flooding the trees.
In the twinkling of an eye. Two points of light I swung

on him and he blinked, unfolded in it like a listener in music.
I told him mine and then he knew the family.
I could smell the alcohol. The scorched rubber began to stink.
He'd heard my car racing on the road past his house
at a blank howl (at nights after rehearsals). He wanted
to admire *my car*, see the double-throated carburettor,
the gaping extractors and the howling music of my *exhaust.*

I was so relieved I pretended that I liked him
I tried to be warm and with-it when I was utterly cold
with a head-horror like Kafka's affect with no cause,
seeing his mates in the car, legs sticking out
both side doors, a black-clad carapace, hit-men
or cockroach. I became the stranger, the local
who has left and then returned. Afterwards,
as they drove away, I felt lost in the loosening
shudders of adrenalin ... the blind licence of it.

Make straight in the wilderness, a highway

Their Camp and Herd

In their
country the old sun does things
in every work-shift – of fading colours,
check shirt, blue singlet, jeans and boots
as faded as the beard, the hair.
Ecce Homo.

Second thing:
the dust-white four-wheel drives
and women in green and orange fashion
and men in fluoro or tradie space-suits.
In their other planet they can
breath the air of.

Then single
men whose country gait is casual
and a swagger and even without horses a cliche
worsening you, to be naming it:
on him, on them. Fading
like everything else.

Carrying inside
at last work shift, slabs of beer, Bacardi mixers,
everything drunk from the neck in the throat
in sub-sets of working and drinking,
barcodes of Friday night.
Their eyes when asleep.

By sunset
all the camp gardens are bloody
with hakea blossom, and dizzy rows of drone-
flies are guzzling in the ground-level sunlight
or gossiping zig-zag in lamp-shine.

Later
the rain, and as slowly in memory
as the moments becoming general, this rain
and night falling in the glow of lamps, this
you are fully familiar with but have no
name for. This more like melancholy
than melancholy.

The Hotel of When-it-was

It is changing but changing like stills and merges.
Rooms fade and dissolve, the world of this hotel
bang in the guts of the city with wild creatures
in Rousseau figurations. Wild is only the children's
book term, these creatures are not eating anyone,
the snakes boiling over the edge of pit are hardly
striking, they seem to be on errands but not
running them. Macaws unsettle me with their
can-opener beaks they point rather than clamp.
Jardin. Le cour. L' atelier where the clog maker
cobbles for Van Gogh, and Arles and crows, sunflowers
blaze from doorways like hallucinations.

Between the wars, cold water ran dirty in these basins.
Hot was a memory, the stand-up bidet faced
away from the dishevelled beds. Not movies,
TV series. Shadows, porcelain, lots of brown cloth.
Now few remember, so a fiction
based on a fiction based on research
makes it up. We have been disagreeing, my thoughts
are in the mail, there by telegram, words with stops
worded between them. War declared, no stops.
Now SMS odd poems untaught tautological but no
gassing in brown vans, or being marched off
to trains in your suits and hats and carrying cases.

Upstairs the writer, a muso, a poet, an historian
not attached to the University or sacked
for being cantankerous or not corporate enough,
remembers rooms full of cigarette smoke, decades
of smoking over keyboards, a glass of schnapps,
the ashtray brimming. But wi-fi's a winner isn't it?
Scrolling, dragging, all that. Prodding in the haze
is seriously analogue. The world's abstract
and you're part of it, the idea of you is the idea
of plurality and relativity, no one dies in a back room
for beliefs, just lack of them, briefly, online.
The bottle sinks, the euro squeals but resists.

Hotel Australia is turning Right in this street,
except for Human Rights which were wiped right out
unless for Freedom to Offend as Free Speech, to sneer,
to lie arrogance into your cheeks.

Below on the street, taxis, taxi-cabs, trams
and buses, hit men in cars with their biographers anxious
beside them, or slim boys on scooters aiming 9mm fingers.
Oh blind me. What can I be thinking? I'm sad.
I want to be in love. I want love as real as the art of it.
They say the www of us is data. The muse is a calculating
bitch, celebrity is blank as pop. Troll. Celebrity Reality
is the rhyme 'to be'. I'm really just so proud of my achievements.
Are you on my list? Did you get my test?
I was a legend!

The Hands

for Miska G

Raising my hand
is proof of my continuum: desire as an idea of my hand lifting
and my hand lifting.

Under my hand
is the floored-over world of routines, habits my limbs and mouth
think are their own.

Even the lazy are hard
at work on this lifelong act, unpaid unless on stage as repertoire
and screen, mirroring us.

There's a hand behind me
lifting when I lift but I cannot see it: the poetry is not in us but
around us, said an ageing poet.

I shall grow older,
and other, wear chequered patterns, caps, part my hair lower,
cease looking at the world.

I'll sing until the boards
knock, and the days of hammering at words lined up like nails
drive into the flesh.

Expansion: a Romantic Ghazal

He shuffles a lot, standing or moving off. He is the tram
with its doors shut. A woman rushes up and bangs on the side.

The questions she asks are obvious. Can I? Why won't you?
Just who do you think you are?

Well, if he knew, he'd open the door. And if he knew
her more he'd shut it again. He is so weak opening seems

like seizure. So instead of weak he seizes his doors shut
to save himself. But Oh the universe is expanding. He feels it.

When he stops outside an old house that has broken its hip,
that has two cancerous slates burnt from its roof...

There she is, waiting for him. He takes her for a glass of wine
to stop her shaking her fist. She gets drunk on two and takes

the barman's number on her memory. Of course she does,
the he of this romance is a twat. The universe is not expanding.

The old house clears its throat, it slumps. She is not for opening,
or not for him. Salom, he shouts, this is all your fault!

Acknowledgements

Sky Poems was first published by FACP in 1987, and was the recipient of The British Airways Commonwealth Poetry Book Prize in London, 1987. It also won the Western Australian Literary Prize for Poetry, 1988.

The Well Mouth was first published by FACP in 2005 and re-published by Puncher & Wattmann in 2012. It was a Poetry Book of the Year in the *Sydney Morning Herald* and *Adelaide Review* and shortlisted for the South Australian Festival John Bray Award for Poetry.

Individual poems in Alterworld have previously been published in *The Age, Australian Poetry Journal, The Best Australian Poems 2012* ed. John Tranter, *The Best Australian Poetry* ed. Judith Beveridge, *Between Yes and No, Eureka Street, Mascara Literary Review, Westerly, The Wombats of Bundanon* ed. Kit Kelen.

Lines 57-58 on p.240 of 'At the Disused Drive-in' are from Primo Levi's *The Drowned and the Saved.*

www.ingramcontent.com/pod-product-compliance
Lightning Source LLC
Chambersburg PA
CBHW021139090426
42740CB00008B/848